Paper
Quilting

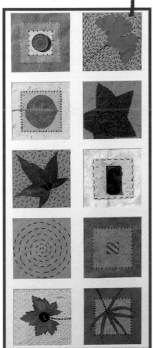

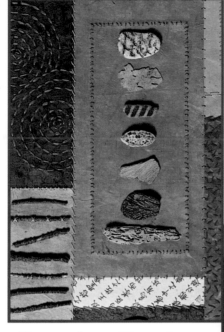

Paper Quilting

Creative Designs

Using Paper &

Thread

Bridget Hoff

Sterling Publishing Co., Inc. New York

A Sterling/Chapelle Book

Chapelle, Ltd.:

Owner: Jo Packham
Editor: Laura Best

Photostylists: Jo Packham and Jill Dahlberg
Photography: Kevin Dilley for Hazen Imaging
Graphics: Kim Taylor
Staff: Areta Bingham, Kass Burchett, Ray Cornia,
Marilyn Goff, Karla Haberstich,
Holly Hollingsworth, Susan Jorgensen,
Barbara Milburn, Karmen Quinney,
Caroll Shreeve, Cindy Stoeckl,
Sara Toliver, Desirée Wybrow

Library of Congress Cataloging-in-Publication Data Available

Every effort has been made to ensure that the information in this book is accurate. However, due to differing conditions, tools, and individual skills, the publisher and author cannot be responsible for any injuries, losses, and/or other damages which may result from the use of the information in this book.

10 9 8 7 6 5 4 3 2 1

A Sterling/Chapelle Book

Published by Sterling Publishing Co., Inc.
387 Park Avenue South, New York, N.Y. 10016
©2002 by Bridget Hoff
Distributed in Canada by Sterling Publishing
c/o Canadian Manda Group, One Atlantic Avenue, Suite 105
Toronto, Ontario, Canada M6K 3E7
Distributed in Australia by Capricorn Link (Australia) Pty. Ltd.
P.O. Box 704, Windsor, NSW 2756 Australia

Printed and Bound in China
All rights reserved

Sterling ISBN 0-8069-4560-5

If you have any question or comment, please contact:

Chapelle, Ltd., Inc.
P.O. Box 9252
Ogden, UT 84409
Phone: (801) 621-2777
FAX: (801) 621-2788
e-mail: chapelle@chapelleltd.com
web site: www.chapelleltd.com

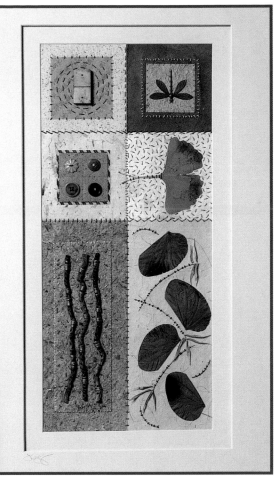

Table of Contents

Introduction

The history of working with paper in art development has evolved over time. Two-dimensional collages using newspaper clippings, colored papers, wallpapers, and wrapping papers have developed into beautiful works of art. Once the potential of collage was recognized, many artists brought their unique talents into the medium. Found objects, paints, and natural elements were added and personal touches flourished. Projects became individual expressions of the artist with the additions of personal effects such as letters, tickets, and cards. Soon tracings and rubbings were explored, followed by the peeling and tearing of papers.

Just as collage has a rich history, needlework and quilting have been enjoyed for generations. Artists have recently taken both of these beloved techniques and combined them into beautiful paper-quilted designs. From traditional quilt blocks to creative collages, quilting and sewing have been used to create beautiful works of art with a combination of diverse mediums and talents. A few of these combinations are showcased in this book.

"I enjoy the idea of quilting with paper because it takes one step out of the "box" and puts quilting in a different light. I love nature, and paper is such a good partner for the natural elements I use—leaves, twigs, and rocks. Using paper and thread gives me a creative way to use my inspiration and the elements of nature to convey the creative spirit and tell the story inside of me to share with the world." Bridget Hoff

General Instructions

Needles & Threads

Decisions for needle size and floss or thread characteristics must take many factors into account. Among them are the weight and texture of the papers that will be pierced and laced through; the colors of both papers and threads in terms of contrast and harmony; the theme and aesthetic "mood" or "tone" of the project; and the skill and patience of the artist to make consistent stitch patterns through layers of paper.

Use the smallest needle possible considering the thickness of the paper and the size of the thread. Available needles to consider are "sharps" which are strong needles with round eyes, used for hand-sewing. Embroidery or crewel needles are sharp needles with long oval eyes. They are used to stitch thin papers. Darning needles are long strong needles with large eyes. They are used for

basting and working with heavy threads. Chenille needles are long-eyed needles with sharp points. They are used for stitching with heavy threads.

Sewing thread without wax, embroidery floss, and metallic filaments can be used effectively for paper. Since wax can discolor delicate or highly absorbent papers, threads without wax are preferred for areas of a project where they will come into direct contact with the paper. Beads strung on waxed thread will stand up away from the paper, but care must be taken where the waxed portion passes through the paper. Thread materials may include: cotton, linen, wool, silk, metallic, natural, manmade, and metallic fibers.

Embroidery floss with its range from brilliant to soft-tinted colors is a harmonious companion to the colors selected for paper-quilt shapes. Because floss can be divided into its separate threads, and because it can fray when being repeatedly pulled through a rigid or fibrous paper, it is essential to test materials at the planning stage. Pull a variety of floss strands and numbers of combined strands (perhaps in different colors) through the papers you plan to use to see how they hold up with repeated lacing.

Cutting Tools

Dedicate a good pair of scissors exclusively for cutting paper.

Decorative-edged scissors are available in a wide selection of designs. These scissors have two edge directions, depending on how they are held. Sharp craft knives used with a ruler are also helpful.

Tips for Supplies:

Be certain that the scissors and needles dedicated for working with paper are not used on other materials.

Store supplies for paper quilting together and separate from those for other types of projects. Then, when beginning a new paper-quilting design, your resources are already gathered and accessible. Tools and needles used with paper are usually unsuitable afterward for fabric, ribbon, and so forth.

Pens, Pencils & Markers

Use writing and drawing tools for embellishing. Be certain pens and markers are fade- and waterproof. Pencils, particularly colored pencils, come in lead, wax, and clay-bound varieties. Experiment with each on scraps of the papers you have chosen for your project. Ideally, you can do this step in the store before you purchase your favorite pencil type. Pens are available in countless colors and with several different tips. Before creating tiny accents and clean lines with them, test them on scraps of your selected papers for how they do or do not bleed. The softer, more absorbent the paper, the more bleeding occurs, which results in a loss of control of detail. There are permanent and nonpermanent varieties, which will give different effects. Do include the metallic—gold, silver, and copper—as well as opaque white pens in your experimentation.

Adhesives

Applying adhesives to paper may cause the sides of the paper to curl. When using lighter-weight materials, such as watercolor paper or mat board, first coat the back side of the material with an acrylic medium to help prevent warping. Once framed, the piece will lie flat.

Use a high-quality adhesive that is user-friendly and easily obtainable, such as gesso, decoupage medium, or tape. To avoid adding excess moisture to paper, use the proper adhesive for each material.

Tips for Adhesives:

Cellophane tape, masking tape, rubber cement, spray adhesives, and mucilage are some artists' preferences.

Hot glue and two-part epoxy can be used under special conditions, but are not considered archival. Hot glue will not maintain its integrity in heat and cold.

Epoxy will turn amber-colored, so use it only where it will not be visible, as with pebbles, metal pieces, or opaque glass.

Select an adhesive that contains little or no water and dries quickly. It is unnecessary to use a wet adhesive for basic paper layering—use a tape-like adhesive. A variety of brands are available that are acid-free, nonyellowing, and heat-resistant. The difference is the ease of use and preference.

Also be conscious of the materials you are securing. Use a stronger adhesive to secure pebbles and glass than you would use to adhere lightweight papers together.

Papers

Select papers with the greatest diversity to achieve the most creative benefit. Consider each piece of paper and how it will best enhance the overall effect of your planned quilting project. Each piece of paper is unique according to its aesthetic qualities. Papers almost speak to you about how they would best be used in a particular artwork. It is not unusual for artists to save a piece of special paper for several years before it finds its way into the perfect collage or paper-quilting project.

Handmade papers can be created or purchased. Their characteristics are as varied as the materials used to make them. The thickness of the paper and its embedded fibrous textures determine how opaque, translucent, or transparent the finished paper will be. Transparent overlay papers make stitching into or near delicate nature materials successful.

Sizing and flexibility of the papers, as well as their thickness and what they are made of, will affect the way adhesives, paints, and inks work on their surfaces.

Paper-like Materials:

Exotic paper-like surfaces may include papyrus, bark, rayon, and metal foils. These surfaces do not take adhesives as well as traditional paper. With suitable mounting products and techniques, and stitching to secure them to their backing, paper-like materials can be successfully incorporated.

Nature materials such as leaves and rose petals can be seen through some transparent papers for a soft effect.

Found Objects

Artists have a passion for certain found objects that they find beautiful, intriguing, and inspiring. Finding such treasures normally takes years of searching, then storing until they find just the right home for each object.

Whether the artist enjoys collecting beads, antique buttons, seashells, or postcards, the found objects available are countless and their use in artwork are becoming more popular.

Colors

The use and mixing of colors in quilting is an essential part of the process of creating. Color can set the mood from bright and happy to somber or sophisticated.

Color is described by defining the hue, or color name; the value, or lightness and darkness; and the intensity, or strength, of a color. Create variety within an overall color scheme by blending different hues of the same value together.

Use intermediate colors to connect widely contrasting ones. Tie a dull red and a bright yellow together by using a midvalue orange. Notice how differently the colors shown in the photography below react with the gray background.

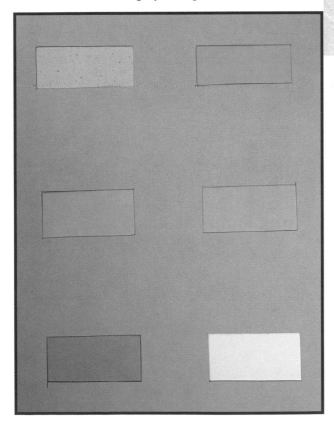

Tips for Working with Colors:

To jazz up a color scheme, include a bit of the complementary color with a dominant color, such as red to green, or orange to blue.

To make a light color appear brighter, place it against a dark background of the complementary color—yellow will appear brighter next to purple than if placed next to orange.

Hot colors such as red attract attention. Cold colors such as blue increase the sense of calm. When placed together, cold and hot colors vibrate like fire and ice.

Light colors such as pale pastels suggest airiness, rest, and liquidity. Dark colors containing black in their composition make the space seem smaller. Combining darks and lights together is a common and dramatic way to represent the opposites in nature such as night and day.

There is no right or wrong on how to use color. Color use is a product of both fashion and tradition, heredity and environment.

Train yourself to see color by looking and being aware of your surroundings. Inspect leaves and flowers; notice how many colors are actually present. A purple pansy may have bits of green and yellow as complementary colors. The sky is filled with shades of blue.

In your paper selection be conscious of the colors and textures and how they relate to the other materials used in your project.

Embroidery Stitches

Straight Stitch

Bring needle up at A; go down at B, forming a straight stitch the desired length.

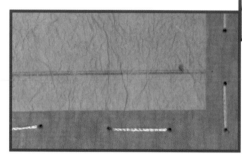

Running Stitch

Bring needle up at A; go down at B creating a straight stitch. Come up at C; go down at D leaving a space between B and C. Continue keeping stitches equal in length.

Whipstitch

Bring needle up at A, go down at B creating a straight stitch. Run needle under completed straight stitches without piercing paper.

Couching Stitch

Bring needle up at A. Stitch over existing thread and go down at B. Repeat keeping stitches evenly spaced.

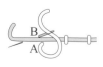

Algerian Eye

Working clockwise, come up at A and down at B. Always stitch into the center.

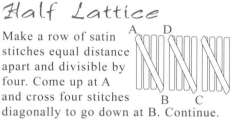

Satin Stitch

Bring needle up at A; down at B, forming a smooth straight stitch. Bring needle up at C; down at D, forming another straight stitch that slightly overlaps the previous straight stitch. Repeat to fill design.

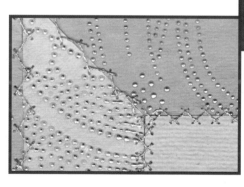

Herringbone Stitch

Working from left to right, bring needle up at A; go down at B. Bring needle up at C, taking a small horizontal backstitch, go down at D. Continue working, alternating from side to side.

Half Lattice

Make a row of satin stitches equal distance apart and divisible by four. Come up at A and cross four stitches diagonally to go down at B. Continue.

Long-arm Cross-stitch

Make straight stitches in a row up to ¼" apart. Come up again at A in the same hole as the straight stitch. Skipping over one straight stitch, go down at B. Come up again at C. Go down at D. Repeat.

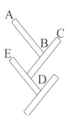

Open Fishbone

Bring needle up at A, down at B. Come up at C, down at D. Come up at E directly vertical to A. Continue

Cross-stitch

Bring needle up at A; down at B, forming a straight stitch. Continue to fill line. Bring needle up at C, cross previous stitch with an equal-sized stitch; down at D. Continue.

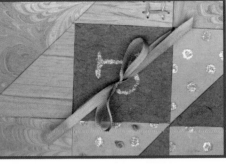

Blanket Stitch

Working from left to right, bring needle up at A; hold thread down with thumb and go down at B emerging at C. Bring needle tip over thread and pull into place. The bottom line formed should lie on the seam line; keep vertical stitches straight and even.

Buttonhole Stitch

Similar to the Blanket Stitch, but stitches are placed closer together.

Feather Stitch

Come up at A, go down at B, and emerge at C. Alternate stitches back and forth, working downward in a vertical column.

Cretan Stitch

Working from left to right, come up at A and down at B. Come up at C, crossing over previous stitch. Go down at D and up at E. Continue. Be certain thread stays under needle to keep an "x" shape.

French Knot

Bring needle up at A. Smoothly wrap floss around needle once. Holding floss securely off to one side, go down at B near A. Do not allow knot to pass through material.

Lazy Daisy Stitch

Bring needle up at A. Go down at B as close to A as possible, but not into A. Bring needle tip up at C and form loop around needle. Pull needle through and go down at D.

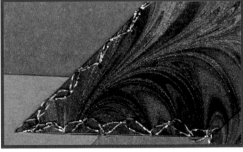

Zigzag Chain

Come up at A, form a loop, go down at B. Emerge at C bringing needle tip over loop. Repeat stitch alternating angles to form a zigzag chain.

Japanese Ribbon Stitch

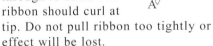

Come up at A. Lay ribbon flat on piece, pierce ribbon in center at point B. Gently pull needle through to back. The ribbon should curl at tip. Do not pull ribbon too tightly or effect will be lost.

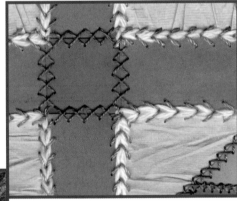

Wheatear Stitch

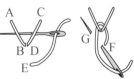

Work from top to bottom, or from left to right. Come up at A and down at B. Come up at C and down at D. Bring thread up a consistent distance down at E and slide needle under previous stitches. Bring needle down near E at F. Bring up at G. Continue.

15

Bridget Hoff

I was born in Laguna Beach, California, to German immigrant parents. My father was a goldsmith and owned his own jewelry store, and my mother ran the home and the business. I was influenced by both parents in many different creative ways. Being a jeweler, my father was detail-oriented in his work and was drawn to the contemporary style of his craft. My mother was quite a good seamstress and was continually doing some type of handicraft, whether it was sewing or embroidery.

When I was a child, my father did a fine-art show that would run for six weeks every summer. This became my playground for those summer days. I was strongly influenced by the artists and their work and the skills required to sell one's work. At the age of seven, I sold my first piece in my dad's jewelry store. By the time I was in high school, I was in a wonderful art program in my school and spent every moment I could in the art room. There we did every sort of craft except drawing and painting.

My medium was "fiber" and I had a wonderful teacher who gave me great latitude to "do my own thing." In my 20s, I became interested in paper and started to make wall pieces and jewelry from handmade paper. At the age of 24, I started to do the same summer art show that my father had done years prior, and I have been doing shows ever since. At the age of 25, I opened my own picture-framing business and continued to make my art and do shows. After seven years, I sold the business and have been a full-time artist ever since. I would like to interject that I never attended college and that all the techniques I have used over the years, I have developed myself. I am very proud to say that I'm self-taught.

I have not always worked in paper quilting. In fact, my focus has changed a number of times as I have experimented and explored. I love bringing together the different techniques I have learned along the way to create beautiful and unique pieces.

I have always been fascinated with kimonos and their shapes. For years I used the kimono idea exclusively in my creative work in three-dimensional wood sculptures and paper designs like the ones shown at right, on the facing page, and below.

The collage series was made from rice paper attached to a ⅜" particle-board shape, then painted. In this series, I began to use leaves in my artwork for the first time.

Tips from Designer:

If I am working on a project that did not turn out the way I planned, I keep it until a later day. Oftentimes, I am pleasantly surprised at the new technique or inspiration the mistake brings to my mind.

There is rarely a right or wrong way to proceed when developing and honing your inspirational pieces. Since I learn primarily from experiments and making mistakes, I do not throw anything away.

After developing a number of collage pieces, I began incorporating vintage objects that I had collected into my pieces, from buttons to skeleton keys to dominos as shown above.

My husband was a sculptor who worked in a wood shop. It was at that time that I began constructing kimonos out of wood. I later added doors to a wooden kimono box holding many treasures. The found objects I added to them made the pieces rather whimsical.

18

Ever since I was a child, boxes as little hiding places have intrigued me. So I took the domino look I used in my kimonos and created a series of domino boxes as shown above, using vintage dominos for the bodies and rusted shell casings for the legs. The tops are particle board covered in antique kimono silk. The cone-shaped tops are Bakelite® buttons. The left box above has a knob from an old iron with a carved-horn feather attached. The insides of the boxes are lined with antique kimono silk.

I ended up creating and selling a wide variety of wooden boxes, as shown at left, in all colors, shapes, and embellishments at craft shows nationally.

From the tiny boxes I was selling at craft shows, I moved into making larger boxes for storage. I have always found peace and comfort in the shape of a house and I incorporated this shape into my larger boxes such as the jewelry box shown here.

In my "house" jewelry box, every pair of earrings I own can be displayed on the wall.

It frees up drawer space and brings me enjoyment because I can see my earring treasures.

In the small purses hanging next to it, I employed stitching techniques that I have also used on paper quilting projects.

During the many years I worked with wood, my interest in jewelry and in boxes prompted me to produce a line of whimsical jewelry boxes and sculptures as shown at the right. They were sold to galleries across the United States.

When I became pregnant with my son, it became apparent that the woodshop and my new shape were incompatible. I realized also that the wood dust was not healthy for me or for my baby. It was time to change courses again.

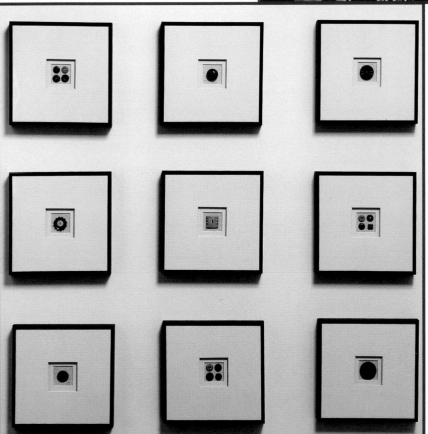

Over the years I had been adding to a collection of found objects. My love for and appreciation of vintage objects has led me to numerous flea markets and antique stores. I decided to display some of my favorite items.

Among my treasures were a number of fabulous vintage handmade buttons. What was needed was a beautiful way to display them. I was inspired by the Amish "nine-patch" quilt design, the simplest quilt pattern. It is the pattern taught to the daughters when they first learn to quilt. The natural progression for me was to create little framed boxes as shown at left to show them individually and collectively on a wall within a nine-patch arrangement.

The progression of my different art phases to being an artist mom has led me to the work I am doing now. Time for creative pursuits must be juggled with my nurturing and practical responsibilities. My work is a way of life. Paper quilting is an ideal activity that lends itself well to my son's needs and my own.

I take my supplies with me to the park or the beach. Working on one square at a time enables me to do something that I can put down at a moment's notice. That way I do not have to worry about paint or glue that dries inconsistently. When all of the squares are complete, I can combine them into one paper-quilt design or frame them individually as shown below.

When my baby was small, I would put him in a backpack, wrangle up my dogs, and head out to go leaf collecting. It was our little project, making money and getting in shape at the same time. Now when it is time to collect leaves, it's still a family affair.

Once home with my leaves, I press them and create cards, boxes, or framed art. Now that I am a single mom to a wonderful five-year-old boy, I am grateful that my craft has been a pleasurable livelihood for me and for my family. I wake every day eager to do what I love. I am truly blessed.

Bridget's Instructions

The basic supplies I use for paper quilting are commonly found around my home. Though this craft requires precision, it is not an exact science requiring particular materials. Whenever necessary, I improvise.

Suggested Supplies:

Craft knife
Craft paper
Fingernail polish remover or liquid acetate
Foam-core board, ³⁄₁₆" thickness
Leaves, seeds, twigs
Needles, assorted
Papers
Pencil
Plastic triangle
Ruler, 24"
Scissors
Spray adhesive
Straight pins
Threads
White glue

And especially—an imagination

Tip for Cutting:

Investing in a small paper cutter will save time in measuring and cutting. You will be at less risk of cutting yourself with the straight edge than with a craft knife.

Needles & Threads

The variety of needles I use is easy to find; any craft store or sewing shop will have what you need. I buy specialty/craft needles in ten-assortment packs. The varieties of needle shaft and eye sizes in these packs provides me with large needles for punching the initial holes and finer needles for the actual stitching. Another convenient pack feature is the graduated assortment.

I like to use cotton thread. Though you may prefer wool or silk, cotton thread is always available and affordable. I look for thread with a bit of sheen to it because it looks so nice against the matte-finish rice papers that I use. Crochet thread is another choice that I sometimes use.

You can use a variety of threads in the same project. I prefer heavy-weight threads for papers and attaching found objects. However, for pressed leaves, extra care must be taken, and heavy-weight threads may not be appropriate.

Background Materials

Use your imagination when selecting materials. Consider items such as:

Fabric
Foreign newsprint
Handmade paper
Maps
Old letters
Receipts
Rice paper
Stationery
Ticket stubs
Wallpaper
Watercolors on any type paper
Wrapping paper

Tips for Working with Papers:

Do not be afraid to work with paper, it is not as fragile as one may think.

To avoid frustration, select a medium-weight paper while learning to sew on paper. Thin papers tear easily, while heavy papers are difficult to pull thread through.

I prefer rice paper because it is fibrous and therefore durable. To use a lacy, rice paper bonded to a colored paper before quilting. This gives the paper added strength and the color shows off the lace pattern.

Be aware that newspaper will yellow with age. Photocopy the newsprint if you wish to preserve the color.

For creating an unusual texture, tightly crumple the paper, then flatten with a hot iron.

Paper is unforgiving. Once you make a hole with your needle, you are committed to that placement. However, do not despair, you can always start over or you can develop a new pattern, technique, or placement from a "mistake."

Work with smaller pieces of paper. When holding a piece larger than 3" square, your material will bend and crease. It is easier to work with smaller pieces and then stitch them all together to complete the piece.

Found Objects

I find most of the diverse objects that I use, like vintage buttons, checker pieces, or dominos, at estate sales, flea markets, and online. I am continually looking for interesting twigs, leaves, seeds, and sticks outdoors, in craft or floral shops, or in specialty import stores. This applies to rocks and pebbles as well.

Part of what I love about my work is that I examine everyday objects for their shapes, colors, patterns, and designs.

When I am walking, I find that I observe people's gardens with an entirely new appreciation.

I tend to group and display my found objects around my home as shown above. This inspires me with new project ideas. It may take some time before an object makes it into a piece of art. Meantime, I enjoy looking at the items.

By collecting, organizing, and grouping various found objects, I can go to work when an idea occurs to me, rather than scurry around trying to find the materials I need.

Collecting Leaves

Leaves are best picked in the fall when their colors are turning, but you can press green leaves as well. When you pick the "turning" leaves, it is best to do so before they hit the ground. Once they are on the ground, they are more apt to be wet. When you press a wet leaf, you run the risk of mildew. However, even mildew can be pretty on certain leaves.

Tips for Picking Leaves:

Pick sycamore leaves in the spring before they grow too large.

Select thin leaves, such as maple, oak, ginkgo, liquid amber, plum, apricot, and lacy geranium. When thick leaves dry, they tend to crack easily when you punch the holes in them.

Do not use leaves that are too thin, such as Japanese maple, for they are too brittle to work with when dried.

Once, I picked hundreds of yellowing ginkgo leaves—it had just rained. Months later when I went to use them, they were all spotted with brown mildew; however, some of them looked quite interesting. I went ahead and used them and was rather pleased with the outcome.

Once you collect the leaves you like, dig out all of your old phone books or any other books that have porous pages. Avoid using magazines or any book with glossy pages—they are not absorbent. Place the leaves in the book, skipping about 20–25 pages at a time. Place the leaves face down, this way they generally lie flat better.

Tips for Pressing Leaves:

One pressing technique is a traditional leaf press. These can be purchased through catalogs, but I think they are rather expensive. Additionally, they are fairly small if you are pressing a large number of leaves.

Unless you already have a leaf press, my old telephone book method works just as well. Save your money for a nice frame when you are finished with your project.

An alternative option is to purchase dried leaves in craft stores or on the Internet.

Once you have placed all your leaves, there are two "pressing" options. Place a heavy object on top of the book, such as another book, and wait several months; or place the entire book in a microwave oven.

If using a microwave, place about six dinner plates on top of the book to weight it down. Cook on high for 2–3 minutes. Be careful in this process because the leaves can burn. Keep weight on books for a week or two before using the leaves.

The problem with microwaving your leaves is that the integrity of the leaf may be compromised. The leaf becomes thinned and more brittle, thus more difficult to work with. It is better to wait for more predictable and beautiful results.

Tinting Leaves

Once the leaves are pressed and well dried, you may want to color or "tint" them. Over time, some leaves will change color. Sometimes this is pretty, but occasionally it distorts the project. In my experience, green leaves turn brown, yellow leaves may remain yellow or turn an orange-brown, and red leaves generally stay red.

There are several reasons for tinting leaves. Generally, it is done to preserve the original color of the leaf at the time it was collected. For example, I use a number of ginkgo leaves in my work. I love the green color harvested in the spring and the mustardy yellow color harvested in the fall. Generally I tint the leaf with the same color it was naturally.

It is possible to tint only half of the leaf to create an interesting look. An oak leaf, for example may be green on one side of the main vein and yellow on the other as shown at left.

Use your imagination to apply acrylic paints, thinned with water. You could also use oil paints that are found in any art supply store, watercolors, inks, or any other tinting medium you desire. I prefer water-based paints because they are easy to clean up and are not smelly.

Photocopying Artwork

There is no real difference between these paper quilt designs, except that the image below is a photocopy of the original at right.

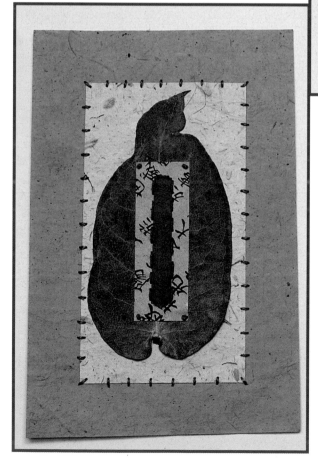

Sometimes I am especially proud of a paper quilt design and want to share it with others. Photocopying a completed piece is quite effective in duplicating artwork.

An additional advantage to photocopies is that the color is permanent—there will be none of the fading that you get with a lot of rice papers.

Tips for Photocopying:

Before adding three-dimensional objects, take your completed pieces to be photocopied.

White tones generally do not copy well. The color comes out with a yellowish cast to it. Brighter colors turn out the best, though it depends on the machine being used.

Long banner-like pieces should be copied in two different sections, then spliced together. Most color copy machines can print up to 11" x 18".

Take your own paper to be copied on. You will then know the quality of the paper.

Be careful not to crease the paper because it leaves a noticeable mark.

Be aware that you can make a large piece from a small image by one of two ways. Have the piece enlarged with the use of the machine or create a pattern that can repeat itself and splice it together.

Use a copy center that does a lot of business; they tend to service their machines every week, which can make a BIG difference in the color quality.

When I start to stitch on a photocopied piece, the process with the needles is the same as an original. I generally follow the same stitch pattern that is on the original piece and stitch over it. On occasion, I add extra stitching to make the piece more interesting.

After I am finished stitching, I embellish with three-dimensional objects as shown at right.

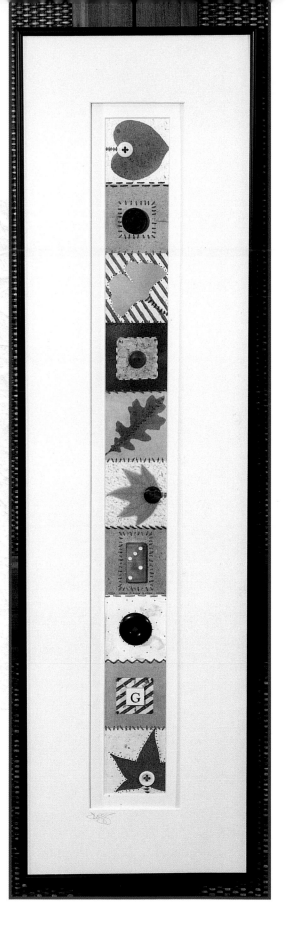

Bridget's Construction

The steps for paper quilting are simple and basic. The embellishments and stitches may change, and the papers and elements may differ, but the technique is the same.

Step 1

Graph out a 10" x 20" foam-core board in a 1" grid such as the Foam-core Grid Diagram at right.

Step 2

Select your desired types and colors of papers. Cut the papers into appropriately sized sections and lay them out on the foam-core grid.

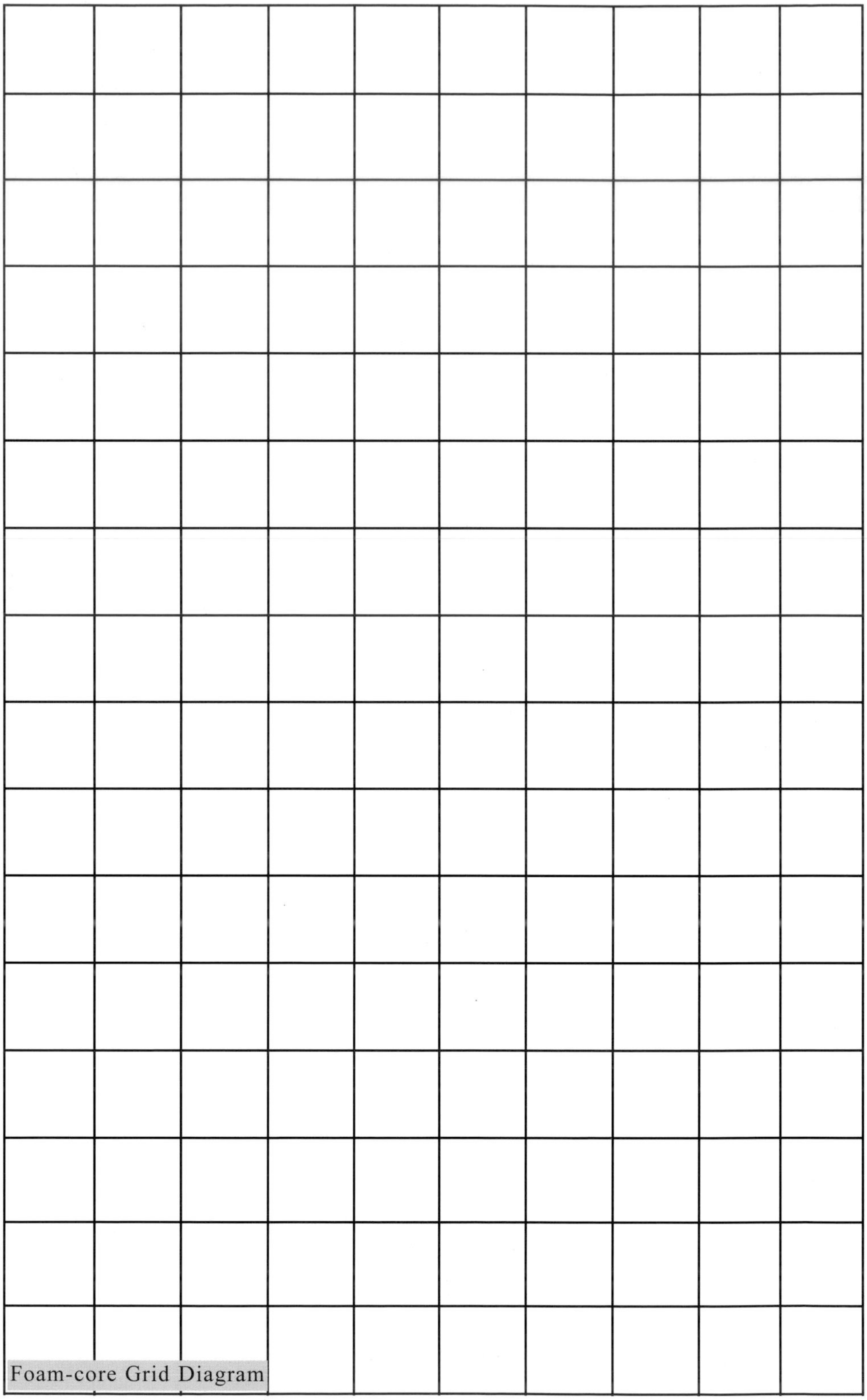

Foam-core Grid Diagram

Step 3

Use straight pins to secure the paper sections to the foam-core grid. Use two pins for each section. Be certain to not press pins all the way through the foam core or you will prick yourself with protruding pins.

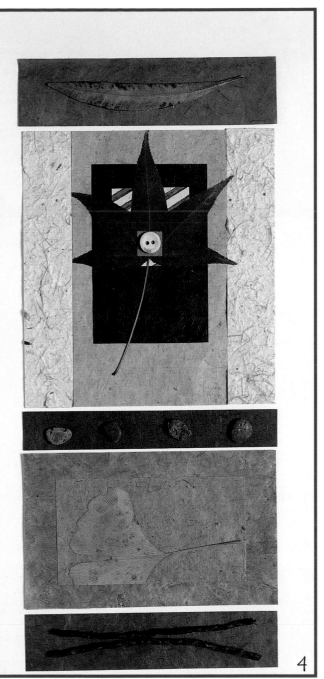

Step 4

Place leaves on sections as desired. Experiment with different positions.

Step 5

When you are happy with the placement, begin gluing. Adhesives can be unforgiving, so practice on some scraps before starting on the project.

You may use different types of adhesive; however, a spray adhesive will give a firm hold and will not pucker the paper like water-based glues.

Now you are ready to adhere your leaf. This is a one-time shot because the leaves are fragile and the adhesive is sticky; so once you have placed the leaf, do not try to lift it back up or move it.

Using white craft glue, adhere a button, sticks, and other found objects onto the sections.

Tips for Gluing:

When gluing, you may get a bit of overspray, so do this part outside or in the garage. Over a large trash can or empty box, hold the leaf vertically in your hand and spray the back side with adhesive.

Do not get the leaf too wet or the adhesive will seep out the side when it is positioned on the board.

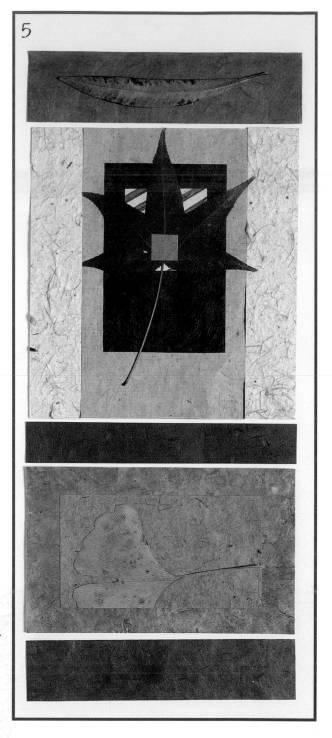

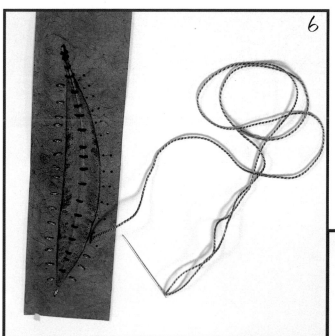

6

Step 6

Once adhesive has dried, you are ready to stitch. With the larger, first needle, pierce holes through the paper and leaves, creating the intended pattern to be sewn. These holes need to be large enough to allow the smaller second needle and thread to smoothly glide through, or the paper will tear.

Step 7

Thread the second needle with appropriate thread. Stitch the leaves and papers together following the pattern. When you have completed one of the sections, pin it back onto the foam-core grid.

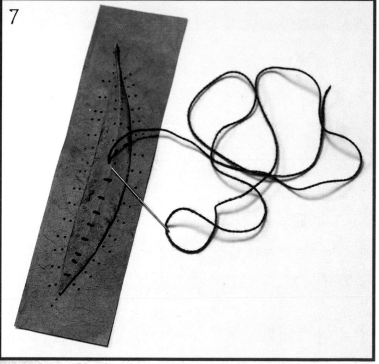

7

Tips for Stitching:

Do not limit your stitch types. There are a number of embroidery and sewing stitches. Develop a variety of stitches you enjoy doing and that are conducive to your desired look.

When mixing stitches, be careful not to have one stitch type or thread type overpower another.

Refer to Embroidery Stitches on pages 12–13. Use a variety of decorative stitches and threads to add textures, colors, and patterns to squares.

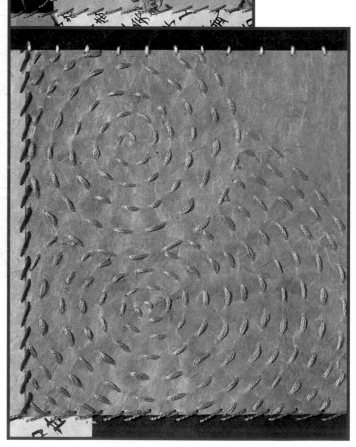

Tips for Embroidering:

Leaves are so beautiful in the way Mother Nature has designed them. Strive to not distract from the leaf itself with the stitching you do around them. Try to "frame" with the stitching to emphasize their beauty.

Quilting strengthens the paper due to the added thread fiber running through it. However, be conscious of how close the stitches are to one another to prevent the risk of the paper tearing.

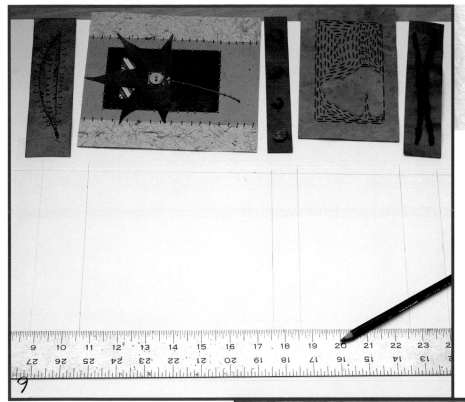

Tip for Gluing:

Bubbles may form when gluing. If you find bubbles, blot them with a piece of scrap paper before they bleed through the paper in your design.

Step 10

Evenly apply a coat of spray adhesive to the graphed paper. A light coat of adhesive will prevent "bleeding" through thin papers. It is best to spray a light coat, wait approximately 30 seconds, then lightly spray another coat. Carefully place stitched sections onto the graphed paper.

Step 9

After completing the hand-stitching, cut a piece of craft paper approximately ¾"–1" larger than the finished project.

Following the Measurement Grid Diagram shown on page 38, graph out the background paper according to the size and shape of your design. Use a measurement grid to keep pieces straight and uniform when applying various squares.

Adhere squares evenly onto paper.

37

A number of my pieces have the same or similar layouts as shown on the Measurement Grid Diagram at right and in the example below. I enjoy working with this long rectangular shape.

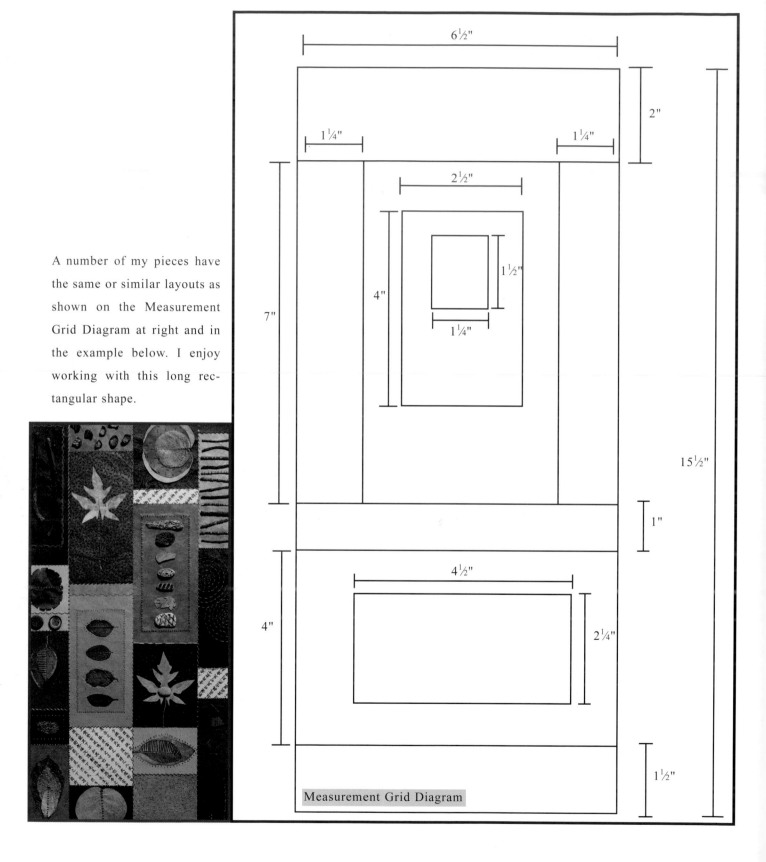

Measurement Grid Diagram

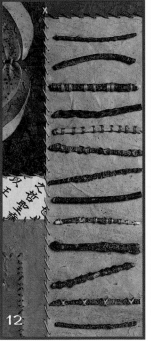

Step 12

When all the sections are sewn together, adhere rocks and pebbles with glue. Secure twigs and sticks with straight stitches.

Step 11

After all of the sections are secured, place them on a flat hard surface and rub firmly, yet gently to be certain they are evenly secured.

Stitch all the sections together like a "quilt." First pierce holes with a larger needle, then stitch the piece with the smaller, threaded needle. Stitch individual squares together first, then stitch rows together.

Step 13

When the design is complete, have it framed as soon as possible to protect the piece. If you take your work to professional framers, bring to their attention that you have used real leaves and that they are very fragile. If you are framing the piece yourself, do not use an air gun. Use a paintbrush to carefully dust off the piece before placing the glass on top.

Tips from Designer:

The piece at right has the same design as the piece above. The only differences are the colors and the embellishments used.

The addition of dominos, buttons, and leaves brings a completely different look to these works.

When working a large project, lay it on a flat sturdy surface to keep paper from creasing while stitching.

Three Rooms

Though my technique is the same through all my pieces, the use of color, form, and objects makes a dramatic change to each piece.

These two pieces depict rooms on a home. This design holds a personal relevance for me, yet I don't make it very often. I am a homebody and find much peace and comfort within a home.

I have always been strongly drawn to the "house" shape. The three windows are significant to me. I've always loved things in sets of threes and, visually, they fit so nicely in this shape.

As with all my pieces, I work on an intuitive level. Most of the time I don't know why I do what I do and I don't contemplate what it "means." I prefer that those viewing my work bring their own meaning (if any) to each piece.

Paper Quilt

The piece below was inspired by the traditional patchwork quilt, made up of same-sized squares of fabric. As with any artist, I put my own spin on it. Here, again, I was drawn to shape, color, and texture, and then I balanced the combinations of elements together.

Assemblage House

The piece above I made years ago when I was heavily into my found-object period. Once again, I am drawn to the "house" shape. In this piece, I have used magazine cutouts, dice, coins, beads, and other treasures.

Banners

During the summertime in the town where I'm from, it is traditional to hang large banners displaying the works of local artists.

Since I have always been drawn to long narrow shapes, I was inspired to make my own banners out of paper. As is my style, such as the banner at the right, I approached them from a design point of view, where color and balance are key.

Many times I use a multicolor palette that works together. Recently, I have enjoyed working with a basically one-color palette, whether it be red, blue, or purple. It's been rather challenging for me, yet quite fun to explore.

Flag

The idea for this piece came from an advertisement in a magazine. It was not the item they were selling, but an abstract painting hanging on a wall in the background that intrigued me. I was drawn to the proportion of the painting. I went into the studio and began to toy with the concept. As I was working on it, the proportions of the piece reminded me of a flag. This gave me the idea of doing a series on flags, and creating my own version of the different flags of the world.

44

Tapestries

My tapestry pieces are more complex for me in design and excitement than other pieces I do. Because of the wide variety of shapes, sizes, and textures of paper, balance becomes much more pertinent. I can have a piece nearly complete and one 1" x 2" section can hold me up because the placement is not right. I redesign my pieces until they feel just right.

The stitchwork on these pieces is quite detail-oriented. The tricky part is their large size. With fabric quilting, you can bend and fold the fabric as you work or you can place it in a large frame. However, with paper, and especially projects with dried leaves, the project must remain flat so the leaves don't crack and break. Therefore, working on the center of large paper pieces is difficult.

Sarah Lugg

Sarah is a British artist who works with mixed media. She lives with her husband in Surrey, England. She was brought up in the beautiful country-side in the south of England, spending her weekends and most of the holidays with her Grandparents on the Isle of Wight. These formative years of beachcombing have greatly influenced Sarah's work today.

After graduating in Graphic Design from Kingston University, she spent her early twenties working as a designer for Sir Terence Conran. Sarah painted and worked on her own style of collages extensively during that time. She now devotes herself purely to her collages and paintings.

Sarah's unique and distinctive style has led to many prestigious commissions and exhibitions. These include sixty collages for the United Kingdom Mission to the United Nations in New York, and a further thirty collages for the British High Commission in Trinidad, as well as commissions from many interior design companies, art galleries, and private collectors worldwide. Sarah is a regular exhibitor in America at Accent on Design in New York, where her shows are always a sellout.

From framed collages to natural elements displayed on tags such as shown at right, Sarah's work has become very popular. It can now be found in the form of posters; a large line of Sarah Lugg stationery including greeting cards, boxed note cards, and card sets; as well as journals and bookmarks. From wrapping paper to totes, and from illustrated poetry books to a line of exquisite wire-edged ribbons, Sarah's work is being enjoyed worldwide.

The latest additions to the Sarah Lugg Collection are a range of stone coasters, T-shirts and sleep-shirts, and a Sarah Lugg calendar. She has also launched a new line of Sarah Lugg Christmas and home accessories, a collection of paper napkins, and a wedding stationery collection.

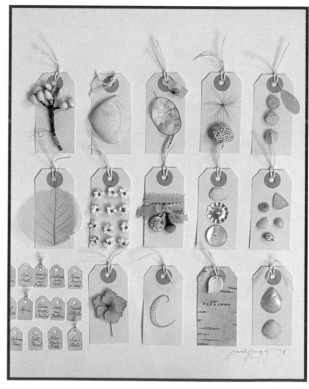

Pia Tryde

46

Sarah was *Victoria* magazine's Artist in Residence for 1999, providing a cover for their February issue, and Sarah's own version of Christmas decorating was featured in their December issue.

"As a small child I was drawn to the hypnotic beauty of nature, always the last to leave the beach as the sun set in preparation for another blissful day for me to explore. Whether it be lost in the watery worlds of stranded rock pools, or disappearing into the woods at the bottom of my parents' garden to wile away countless hours of wandering and wondering in deep contentment, I still find myself totally at peace when immersed within nature. I must point out that I was never lonely, as I shared this time with a very special friend—our Labrador, Honey—one of the finest companions a small child could have.

Pia Tryde

"The world I now share with many people through my paintings and collages is multifaceted and yet one. My childhood collections have grown and now, instead of hoarding them away in boxes, I use them to create my own personal style of mixed-media work, or as inspiration for my paintings.

"I strongly believe in following the flow of thought and energy, and not forcing or prejudicing my work. I want to share my vision with you. The paintings and collages are an evocation of all the pleasures to be found in 'Sarah's World'."

Sarah's Instructions

Sarah's love for the outdoors is incorporated into her works through the natural colors and materials accentuating her pieces.

Suggested Supplies:

Acrylic paints
Bronze powder
Buttons
Candle wax
Crackle glaze
Fabrics:
    sheer
    silk
Flower press
Flowers
Foam-core board
Gesso
Leaves
Metallic papers
Needles, assorted
Oil pastels
Paintbrushes, assorted
Pencil
Permanent adhesive
Ruler
Scalpel
Scissors
Scumble glaze
Seashells
Sea-washed glass
Silver birch bark
Spices, assorted
Threads:
    cotton
    silk
Tweezers
Vintage found objects
Watercolors

Found Objects

Sarah has always been an avid collector of objects, however insignificant they may seem, because she thought they were beautiful. Feathers, seashells, barks, and stones are stored around her home and in her studio along with colored silks, sea-washed glass, leaves, seeds, and scraps of printed paper.

Sarah uses small tags as shown at right as a vehicle for displaying these intricate and intimate treasures that she has been gathering since childhood.

Background Materials

Be creative in the material types and colors you use. Consider items such as:

Bark
Fabric
Foreign newsprint
Handmade paper
Old letters or postcards
Stamps
Tags
Ticket stubs
Tissue paper
Watercolor paper
Wrapping paper

Needles & Threads

Sarah uses an assortment of needles specific for the thread with which she is working. She prefers cotton or silk threads because they are readily available and work well in her projects.

Silk thread is quite durable and picks up color well. Silk also contributes light and luster bringing a subtle glow to a project.

Sarah's Construction

Though the layout of a project may be a basic grid design, personality and inspiration create the art.

Step 1

Graph out on watercolor paper a base pattern, such as the Basic Nine Grid Diagram at right. Add a border if desired.

Basic Nine Grid Diagram

Step 2

Color selected squares and patterns with water-thinned acrylic paint. Let dry. Draw design elements, such as the heart shown, on tracing paper. On back of tracing paper, rub a pencil across the designs. Place tracing paper, with design right side up, over selected square. Trace over the design to leave an outline.

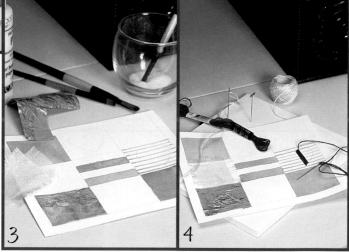

Step 3

Adhere gold foil or any other chosen papers as desired. For added texture, thin gesso with water and wash over paper. Cut selected fabrics to fit squares and fray all four sides. Adhere fabrics to paper.

Step 4

Using T-pin and base pattern, pierce stitching holes where you choose to stitch. Refer to Embroidery Stitches on pages 12–13. Make desired stitches to enhance the piece.

Step 5

Apply glue to desired square before arranging seeds and spices on piece. Adhere chosen flowers and shells.

Step 6

Frame carefully and display as desired.

Adapting the Grid

The Basic Nine Grid is a simple shape to work with and the concept can be easily adapted into different projects.

Using different-sized grids, these pieces have their own personalities. Newspapers, fabrics, sheers, and papers are brought together with complementary colors. Satin stitches and straight stitches help attach some found objects while bringing dimension to the design. Turquoise rocks, leaves, medallions, wrapped wire, berries, and seashells add to the design and color palette.

The five-square grid design as shown at left and the four-square grid design as shown above consist of a combination of papers and fabrics, bringing these colorful pieces to life.

A wide variety of found objects such as feathers, ginkgo leaves, buttons, dried rosebuds, anise seed, hot peppers, postage stamps, and stickers embellish these pieces to enhance the elemental theme.

Sarah collects and uses a myriad of materials that add color and dimension to her pieces. The piece above is made of gold packaging that she cut into squares, then glued together. She then layered fabric over the top and attached it with fine thread.

"My innovative collages are enriched by my unique personal interpretations. I enjoy combining the sophisticated delicacy of ancient Assyrian forms with a deeply sensitive use of color and exquisite finely judged textures."

"I believe that my work has its own particular quality. My life's love for gathering fragments from nature, and my artistic talents and attention to detail convey to the viewer a world with which we are fast losing touch.

"In the work, I try to convey my obsession with the qualities of organic fragments—their shape, form, color, and texture.

"All these elements spark my imagination to a level where my paintings and collages become one.

"I love the spiral shape—its structure and form have always been a major source of inspiration for my work. The spiral, one of the predominant forms to be found in Nature is exquisite, whether it is an unfurling fern or a tiny seashell."

Adapting Found Objects

In the piece above, Sarah was inspired by the rooms of Assyrian sculpture at the British Museum in London. The collage is a montage of painting, stitching, and paper layering. She masterfully added unusual and ordinary found objects.

The broken glass was taken from an old car windshield, then pieced together using tweezers and glue. The other found objects such as feathers, seashells, pebbles, and metal birds have been collected over time and found their home in this piece.

Layering

To create the textured background for these pieces, Sarah washed gesso over handmade paper. She then layered with newsprint, fabric, papers, and tags.

The flower card cutouts at right are attached with straight stitches which enhance the satin-stitched tree. The waves are satin-stitched with a mixture of pearl cotton and embroidery flosses, bringing a different weight into the picture. A combination of shells and glass brings the sea floor to life. Mosaic glass, satin stitches, and a variety of papers create a colorful border.

Placing Seeds & Glass

"My world is a microcosm of all the imagery, colors, textures, and artifacts that have captured my attention during my short journey through life.

"I have always been an avid collector of objects, however insignificant, just because I thought they were beautiful."

Special care is taken when placing small objects such as broken glass bits or seeds. Sarah makes certain to have adequate lighting and a sturdy workplace. She stays focused on the areas she is creating and remains patient, keeping the objects uniform in placement. She patiently lines up each seed, such as the sesame seeds shown above, using a scalpel and tweezers. Broken glass pieces are fit together as snugly as possible.

In her other pieces, Sarah uses this same method when placing such objects as vintage stamps, bits of newspaper, small rosebuds, and lavender.

Tinting

The seashell at lower right is naturally green, but the spiral shell is tinted with a wash of watercolor. The gesso-textured square under the shells is tinted with washes of watercolor and acrylic, then rubbed with oil pastel.

The tinted squares continue the color theme throughout the piece. The collector stamps and large straight stitches are the focal point of this piece. Divers papers and fabrics complement the handwritten letter embellished with rosebuds and seashells.

Nature is also a source of unending influence on Sarah's work. Her paintings take inspiration from the tiny details of texture, shape, and color to be found in the natural elements of her collages. These transformed visions, are given new dimensions, as Sarah experiments with the relationship and relative proportions of images and backgrounds.

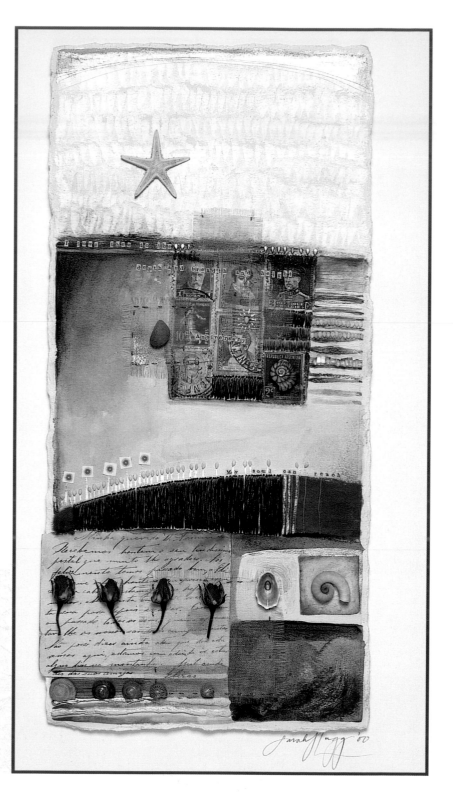

Tips for Ironing Silk:

Silk wrinkles easily. To release wrinkles, place cotton fabric over the silk and press with a cool iron. Do not use spray or steam.

Another way to give silk the appearance of being freshly ironed is to soak it in cold water. Wring it until nearly dry and press it against a mirror. Try to get it as flat as possible to keep out the wrinkles. Spread a dry towel under the mirror, because when the silk dries (within an hour) it will drop off the mirror clean, fresh, and wrinkle-free.

Working with Silk

Silk has a translucency that absorbs and reflects light, giving the finished project a beautiful shimmering luster. Though silk is beautiful in the finished project, it requires special care in handling. When using silk, work in a well-lit area, yet stay out of direct sunlight to prevent discoloration. It is not recommended to wash silk for any project, so keep your hands very clean and free from oils. Be aware that small water spots on silk will leave marks even after drying. Use a light spray adhesive when gluing silks, to prevent adhesive from seeping through the material.

Store silk in an interlocking bag with a small corner cut out of the bottom. This will allow the air to be pressed out, yet still protect against light, air, and insects.

Using Gesso

To create a texture, Sarah applied a layer of gesso to the background. This application helped strengthen the paper to withstand the numerous satin stitches. The gesso also acted as an adhesive in holding the papers, cutouts, and added fabrics. The dots in the center of the piece are made of a combination of gold ink, oil pastels, and gold leaf.

Tip for Design:

When designing, remember things do not have to look a certain way. Note that the knots from the stitches are purposely left on top of the piece shown below rather than hidden on the back.

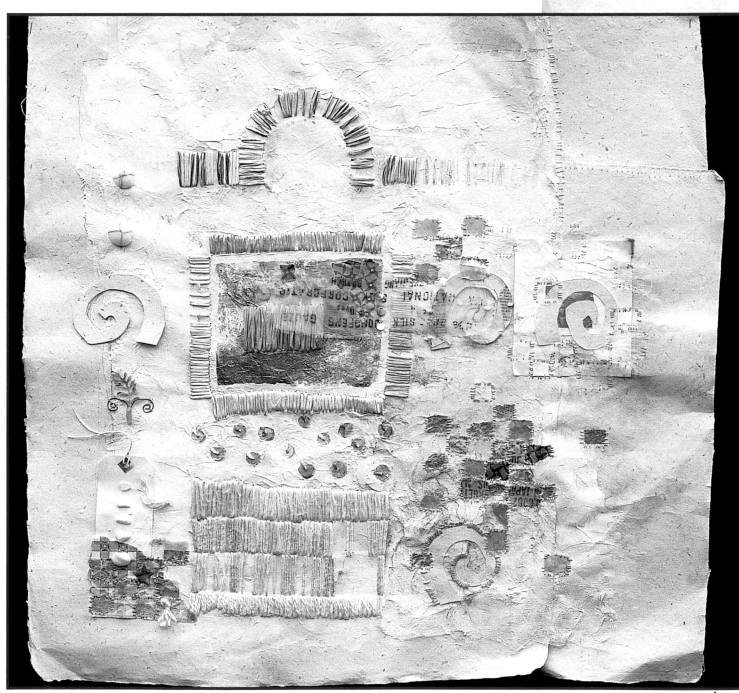

Transferring Photocopies

The shell on the right side of this piece is a photocopy of a real shell, which has been transferred onto the paper and incorporated into this piece with actual shells.

Copy a shell or a colored or black-and-white picture of a shell. Tape the selected project paper on the work surface. Place the photocopy face down on project paper.

In a well-ventilated area, rub a colorless xylene-based-liquid blending marker over the back of photocopy with plenty of pressure. Lift at one corner to check results. The final look will be determined by the amount of fluid from the marker and the amount of pressure applied.

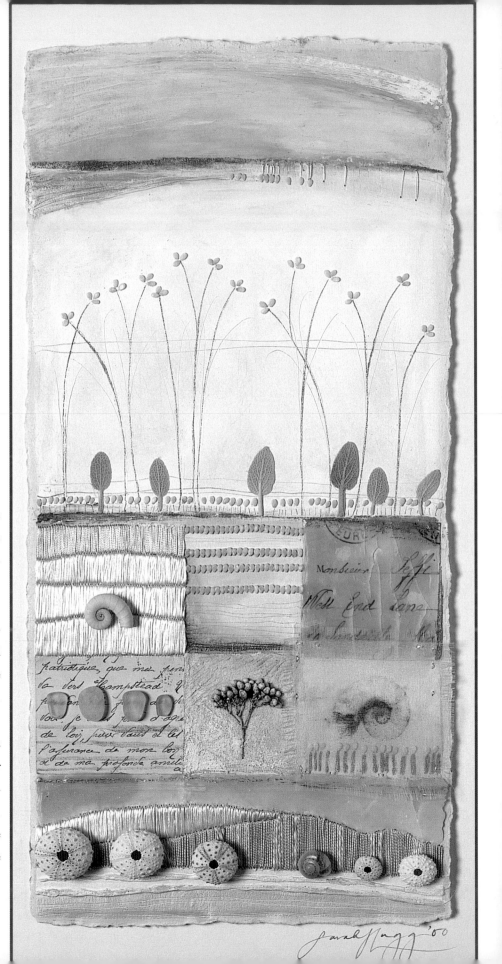

"I always work intuitively, allowing the paintings and collages to grow and develop their own life force. The stimulation may come from a previous piece of work, a small collected item, a line of poetry, or just the accidental fall of objects onto my work bench."

The leaf in the piece below is a transfer. Using a colorless liquid blending marker, Sarah combined a black-and-white photocopy of an actual leaf to the piece below.

Using Melted Wax

These leaves were dipped in a pot of melted wax several times. If the wax is allowed to cool a little, it deposits a thicker coat. When the wax was cooled, it was slightly cracked off of the leaves. Metallic powders were applied using fingertips. Hot wax was also spooned into the bottom left-hand square of the piece below.

"Feathers, shells, barks, and stones introduced into a collage convey a spiritual message that transcends their common origins or diminutive scale.

"The tiniest fragment of nature is endowed with content, symbolism, and spirituality. The words within the work are personal hidden poetry which transfuse it. The messages, which are always private, hide treasures I choose to share with the observer."

Wrapping Threads

Wrapping threads is very time consuming. Be patient and keep the threads uniform and even. When planning to wrap threads around cardboard, be certain that the cardboard is stiff enough to withstand many hours of handling. Keeping the threads uniform around curves is difficult; for this reason, do not attempt corners.

The wrapped wire, the tags, and the gold-sprayed magnolia leaf make up the focal point of the overall piece. Ferns, dried flowers, seeds, feathers, and stickers meld colorfully into the design.

Tip for Design:

Projects do not have to be symmetrical. This piece beautifully displays how the overall piece can tilt, bringing more interest to the design. This technique tends to give the viewer a more fluid feel. Notice that Sarah's signature also is in an untraditional position.

Rhonda Rainey

Working with a myriad of mediums and materials, Rhonda is an award-winning watercolorist, designer, and published author. She has written a number of books on faux finishing and continues to explore the beauty and versatility of combining paper into artwork. Rhonda is passionate about quilting and has found enjoyment in combining a variety of papers, faux-finishing techniques, and quilting into her latest projects.

An art educator for twenty years, Rhonda is currently working as a free-lance artist and designer. She is the mother of three grown children and is a fun-loving grandmother. She resides in Idaho where the rugged landscape and the quiet beauty of nature provide inspiration and subject matter for much of her work.

Rhonda continues to encourage readers, students, and friends to try new materials and techniques and to let their imaginations run wild.

Rhonda delights in the wide variety of papers available. Because it is such an integral part of everyday life, only recently has paper come into its own as an expressive and versatile art medium.

As with her projects, shown above and at left, Rhonda has learned that anything that can be cut or torn and pasted or sewn onto a surface can be used to create a new design.

With the advent of new glues and varnishes, and the availability of exotic and unusual papers, Rhonda considers endless possibilities when choosing materials to accent a special piece.

Rhonda's Instructions

Rhonda primarily works with paints and decoupage medium. She has found that the materials already in her studio are an inspiration when developing and combining different techniques.

Suggested Supplies:

Acrylic paints
Buttons
Coffee filters
Cotton balls
Craft glue
Craft knife
Decoupage medium
Embroidery flosses
Fresh leaves
Lightweight interfacing, nonfusible
Needles, assorted
Paintbrushes, assorted
Paper towels
Pencil
Permanent black marker, ultrafine
Ruler
Scissors
Stylus
Threads
Watercolors

Needles & Threads

It is important to use a needle that coordinates with your chosen thread. Rhonda lets the materials and intended use determine the weight of the needles and threads she chooses.

She is careful when selecting thread colors. On some projects, Rhonda uses a metallic thread to accent the stitches as part of the design. When the stitching is more functional than decorative, she uses white or a muted color so as not to conflict with the project's focal point.

Background Materials

Rhonda experiments with a wide variety of paper materials in her projects.

Brown paper
Card stock
Corrugated cardboard
Homemade paper
Patterned napkins
Perforated paper
Suede paper
Wallpaper

Papers

The majority of papers Rhonda uses is available at craft stores, stationery shops, office supply stores, and supermarkets. The appearance of even the most ordinary papers can be altered by using simple techniques to change their color, texture, finish, and surface.

Even when experimenting, she uses the best quality materials and beautiful stitching, as a test project may turn out to be a masterpiece.

Flowers from India

Supplies:

Acrylic paints:
    antique white
    gold metallic
    gypsy rose
    off-white
    pale beige
    tea rose
    wild rose
Frosted beads, orange/salmon ¹⁄₁₆" (5)
Glue stick
Gold metallic thread, 6'
Papers:
    card stock, 11" x 14"
    handmade, burgundy 4" x 7"
    handmade, dark rose/beige 3½" X 6¾"
    handmade, off-white 4½" x 6"
    scrap, pale leaf design
    suede, burgundy 4" x 6½"
Sponges:
    coarse texture
    fine texture

Step 2

Using fine-textured sponge, sponge-paint envelope with off-white. While off-white is still wet, lightly apply pale beige over off-white. Let dry.

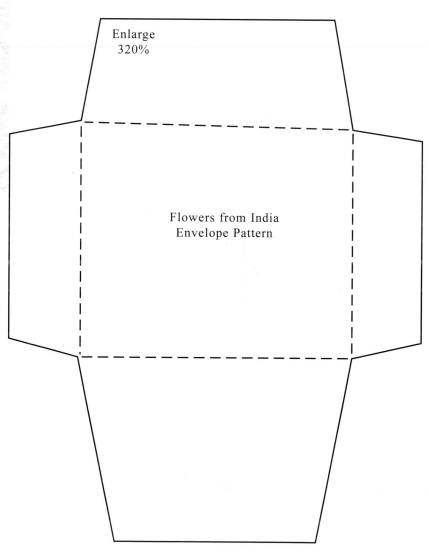

Enlarge
320%

Flowers from India
Envelope Pattern

Step 1

Enlarge and copy Flowers from India Envelope Pattern. Trace envelope pattern onto card stock. Using craft knife and ruler, cut envelope from card stock.

Step 3

Apply a very light layer of tea rose over previously sponged layers. Let dry. Apply gold metallic in a loose random pattern. Let dry.

Step 4

Using coarse-textured sponge, apply a final layer of tea rose over all previously painted areas. Let dry. More metallic gold may be applied to soften look if desired.

Step 5

Using fine-textured sponge, apply pink then gold paints in a fan shape on a piece of white handmade paper.

Step 6

While paints are still damp, gently tear fan shape from paper. Let dry.

Step 7

Repeat Step 6, tearing small shapes for flower's center and edge from burgundy handmade paper. Let dry. Using glue stick, tack shapes together to form the flower.

Step 8

Sew long and short running stitches in fan shape on flower with gold thread. Punch holes at ⅛" intervals with needle. Stitch around edge of leaf design with double strand of gold thread.

Step 9

With single strand of gold thread, sew long and short running stitches around edges of suede paper. Attach beads to flower with gold thread. Using glue stick, tack paper with leaf design to burgundy suede paper. Layer and adhere papers together. Score envelope folds with stylus and ruler. Adhere design to envelope. Weight project with heavy books for 48 hours to avoid curling.

Scrapbook Cover

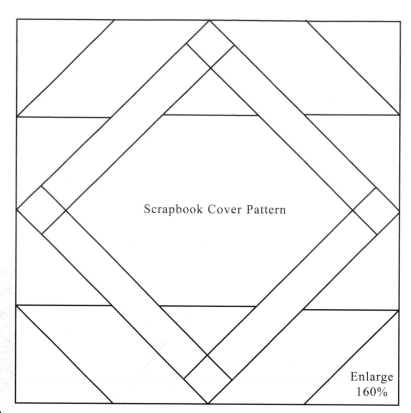

Scrapbook Cover Pattern

Enlarge
160%

Supplies:

Drafting triangle, 12"
Embroidery flosses:
    rose
    yellow-tan
Heavy-weight interfacing, nonwoven
Papers:
    scrapbook, blue marbled 8½" x 11" (2)
    scrapbook, floral pattern 8½" x 11" (2)
    scrapbook, green marbled 8½" x 11"
    scrapbook, striped 8½" x 11"
    suede, rose 8½" x 11"
Quilter's lightweight plastic template
Scrapbook
Waxed paper

Step 1

Enlarge and copy Scrapbook Cover Pattern. Using marker and ruler, trace quilt block design onto lightweight template plastic. Using ruler and craft knife, cut templates from plastic. Using templates and craft knife, cut papers and assemble block according to pattern. Do not glue. Using drafting triangle and pencil, square interfacing. This interfacing square should be 1" larger on each side than quilt block.

Step 2

Begin with center piece of design. Lightly apply decoupage medium to back of papers. Place piece in center of square. Smooth and continue adhering pieces, working from center outward. Trim off excess interfacing. Place block between sheets of waxed paper and weight to flatten. Let dry at least 48 hours.

Step 3

Adhere block to next layer of paper with decoupage medium. Using craft knife and ruler, trim edge ¼" larger than quilt block. With ruler and marker, place dots at ¼" intervals. Refer to Embroidery Stitches on pages 12–13. Stitch French knots at each mark with three strands of embroidery floss.

Step 4

Using triangle, ruler, and pencil, measure and square final layer of paper around edge.

Step 5

Adhere square to album cover with decoupage medium. Coat complete book front with decoupage medium. Let dry.

Tips for Decoupaging:

It is best to practice with any decoupage medium to be certain the materials being used will adhere and remain in place. In general, the heavier the paper, the thicker the medium must be.

Many water-based mediums tend to lose their "tack" when diluted with water. However, many products, unless diluted, are too heavy for lightweight papers. Experiment with different amounts of water.

Corrugated-
Paper Frame

Supplies:

Buttons, ⅜" (5)
Embroidery floss, dark brown
Embroidery needle
Papers:
    corrugated cardboard, 2" x 5¼"
    lightweight, brown 8½" x 11" (3)
    napkin, brown patterned 2¼" x 2¾"
    perforated, beige 14-count ⅜" x 4"
Picture frame, 6" x 6" (2¾" x 2¾" opening)

Step 1

Apply decoupage medium to frame surface to seal. Let dry. Tear three 3" x 11" and two 5" x 11" strips from brown paper. Loosely roll a strip around pencil. Holding paper firmly, push toward center, forming a crimped tube. Remove newly-made paper "spring" from pencil. Unroll and smooth with fingers. Repeat with other strips.

Step 2

Adhere strips to frame, wrapping around edges and frame opening. Take care to maintain crepe-like texture. Cut 2" x 5½" strip from corrugated cardboard. Cut 2¼" x 2¾" patch from patterned napkin. Fold edges under ¼". Refer to Embroidery Stitches on pages 12–13. Using a running stitch, secure patch to cardboard strip with floss, leaving one side open. Do not tie off.

Step 3

Gently push cotton balls into pocket, then stitch closed. Using craft knife and ruler, cut ⅜" x 4" strip from perforated paper. Sew buttons through all layers of paper to secure. Adhere to frame with decoupage medium.

Hollyhock Scrapbook

Supplies:

Acrylic paint, forest green
Folio envelope, 10" x 15"
Leaves, fresh hollyhock or large geranium
Papers:
    card stock, coordinating
    handmade, white 8½" x 11" (2)
    scrapbook, patterned 8½" x 11" (4 designs)
    suede, blue 4¾" x 13"
Waxed paper

Step 1

Cut background papers to form simple patchwork. Apply decoupage medium to back of papers and adhere to folio cover. Be certain edges are neat, flush, and secure. Cover with waxed paper and place under weights. Let dry.

Step 2

Lightly brush green paint on underside of leaves, catching paint on veins. Place white paper over painted surface and rub gently with a folded paper towel to transfer painted design. Remove paper from leaves. Let dry.

Making Yo-yos:

Cut circle of paper. Sew a running stitch around the outer edge. Gather tightly. Knot ends to secure. Slightly flatten puckered circle, pressing tightened gathers to the center. The smooth side is the bottom and the gathered side is the top. Tie off yo-yo.

Step 3

Trim 1" from edges of two coffee filters and 1¾" from two more filters, then discard cut off edges. Paint edges around cut filters and one uncut filter with yellow. Paint band of dark pink inside filters next to yellow, allowing colors to run together. Paint a circle of deep rose in each center, pulling rays of deepest color into pink. Let dry.

Step 4

Float water over transferred surface of leaf. Randomly paint areas with yellow-green, green, and blue, allowing colors to run together. Let dry.

Step 5

Cut transferred leaves from paper, leaving ½" edge. To add texture to the piece, loosely roll paper leaf around pencil. Holding paper firmly, push toward center, forming a crimped tube.

Step 6

Remove newly-made paper "spring" from the pencil. Unroll and smooth with fingers. Repeat with remaining paper leaves, each time rolling paper onto pencil in a different direction. Trim leaves to edges of transfer.

Step 7

Refer to Making Yo-yos on page 82. Form hollyhocks.

Step 8

Cut stem shapes from patterned paper. Adhere stems, leaves, and flowers onto the background as desired. Have yellow center of the flowers visible. Adhere buttons to flower centers over stitching. Using marker, draw stitches as desired. Cover with waxed paper and place under weights for at least 48 hours to prevent buckling.

Vanessa-Ann

Vanessa-Ann consists of a team of talented artists and designers, who create and share a myriad of craft and decorating techniques.

The Vanessa-Ann Collection also known by its parent company, Chapelle, Ltd., has authored and/or copublished more than 150 hardbound titles on subjects ranging from decorating and gardening to master woodworking and antique needlework.

Today, Vanessa-Ann and its top designers continue to provide an endless source of inspirational ideas to consumers requiring the most innovative designs and new product concepts such as these featured on the technique of paper quilting.

With the help of the Vanessa-Ann staff, use your imagination to bring design and beauty into your home through design and color. Explore and create with different papers, stitches, patterns, and design elements.

The paper-quilting projects shared by Vanessa-Ann should be used as a starting place for your own personal works. When your ideas come to life and you enjoy the results with every glance, you have succeeded in bringing imagination into your home in a manner others can enjoy.

Vanessa-Ann's Instructions

Vanessa-Ann continually develops decorating ideas and creates innovative projects. Their studio is filled with supplies used in all facets of painting, stitching, decoupaging, and stamping.

Suggested Supplies:

Beads, assorted
Buttons, assorted
Craft knife
Foam-core board
Gum eraser
Needles, assorted
Papers, assorted
Pencil
Permanent adhesive
Ribbons, assorted
Rocks
Ruler
Scissors:
    craft
    decorative-edged
Seashells
Sewing machine
Small crocheted motifs

Tips for Machine Stitching:

Select stitches that will not pierce the paper so much that it will tear. Keep the stitches far enough apart that the paper is not ripped.

Loosen the sewing machine tension to sew on paper.

Keep a machine needle dedicated for sewing on paper. Change the machine needle between stitching paper and fabric to preserve your materials and the needles.

An important thing to remember when paper quilting with a sewing machine is to take it slow. Unlike fabric, paper is less forgiving. Once a hole is punched, it is difficult to mend.

Needles & Threads

The needles selected are determined by the thickness of the papers and the types of threads used. Other than basic sharp and embroidery needles, Vanessa-Ann designers use chenille needles and beading needles when applying found objects.

The designers at Vanessa-Ann use an assortment of threads including pearl cottons, flower threads, metallic threads, cords, and embroidery flosses. The weight of the thread chosen is based on the thickness of the paper to be sewn, the amount and proximity of the stitches, and the color of thread being used. If a thick thread must be used on a light-colored heavy paper, a soft muted color would be chosen so as not to overpower the design.

Background Materials

When making quilt blocks, the Vanessa-Ann designers use materials that are compatible with each other in color and texture. This is easier to sew and is more pleasing to the eye.

Consider using items such as:

Butcher paper
Card stock
Handmade paper
Marbled paper
Wallpaper
Wrapping paper

Tips for Using a Pattern:

Decide on the pattern to be used. Lightly draw or trace the pattern onto paper with a pencil. Use a T-pin to pierce holes in the desired places before sewing. The T-pin is larger than a needle and the top makes it easy to pull out of the paper.

When piercing the initial holes, set project on a piece of foam-core board or an eraser. This will protect the work surface from pin holes and make a cleaner hole in the paper.

Vanessa-Ann's Construction

Step 1

Collect materials needed for your intended project. Enlarge the pattern you choose to desired size and make three copies. Use one of the copies to cut apart and make a template for the quilt pieces. Keep the second copy for a reference when assembling. The third copy should be copied onto tracing paper to aid in the assemblage. Be careful when using the photocopied tracing paper as it has a tendency to smear. If the tracing paper has crinkled after going through the copier, smooth it out with a cool iron.

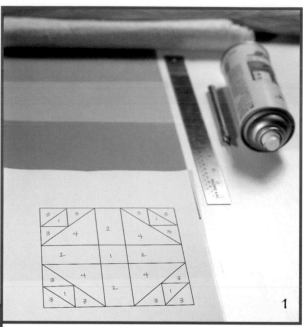

Step 3

Cut out all pattern pieces from selected papers. Be certain to keep lines exact as they will be butted against other pieces.

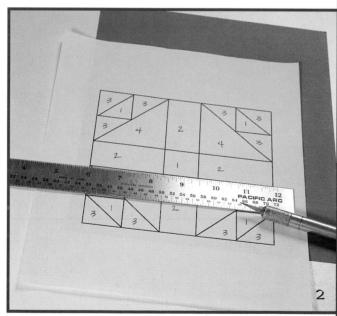

Step 2

Number pattern pieces to coordinate with the different papers you choose to use.

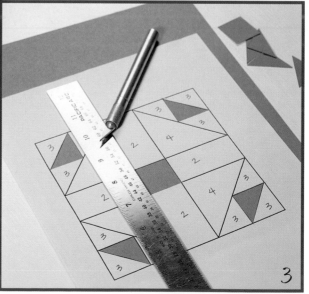

Step 5

Using the second pattern copy as a guide, adhere cutouts onto photocopied tracing paper with spray adhesive. When all cutout pieces have been placed, adhere tracing paper onto background paper. Refer to Embroidery Stitches on pages 12–13. Stitch and embellish.

Step 4

Continue cutting numbered pieces from different colored papers until all pieces are cut out. Whenever you begin working with a new thickness or type of paper, it is best to make a few practice cuts to see how the materials cut and react to your tools.

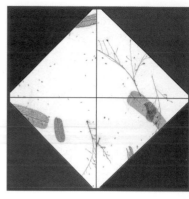

Broken Dishes

Step 1

Enlarge and copy Broken Dishes Pattern onto desired papers. Cut out and assemble pieces.

Step 2

Using machine-zigzag stitch, sew around outer edge of middle square, and around outer edge of entire square.

Step 3

Refer to Embroidery Stitches on pages 12–13. Using sharp sewing needle and same thread used on sewing machine, whipstitch over inner triangles. About 1" from center, make long-arm cross-stitches on all four sides of center.

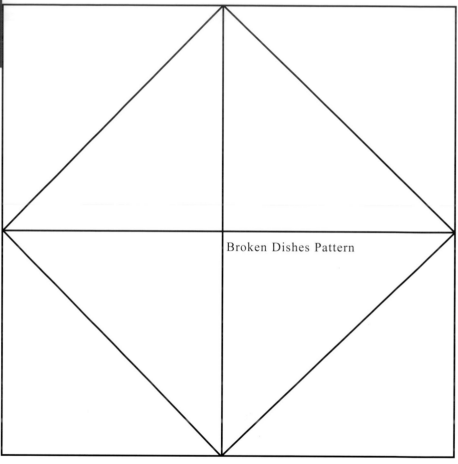

Broken Dishes Pattern

Step 4

Adhere patch onto desired background paper. Using decorative scissors, trim background to fit front of gift bag. Adhere paper to front of gift bag.

Skyrocket Book

Step 1

Enlarge and copy Skyrocket Pattern onto desired papers. Cut out and assemble pieces.

Step 2

Mount square on large sheet of brown handmade paper. Stitch as desired. Adhere square to photo album.

Skyrocket Pattern

Step 3

Tack crocheted heart to square with small hand stitches, going from front to back with coordinating thread. Tack one end of large cord onto top of heart. Lay cord in random pattern on square. Refer to Embroidery Stitches on pages 12–13. Using couching stitch, anchor cord down with coordinating smaller cord.

Mosaic Envelope

Step 1

Enlarge and copy Mosaic Pattern onto desired papers. Cut out and assemble pieces.

Step 2

Mount block on a large sheet of handmade paper. Refer to Embroidery Stitches on pages 12–13. Cretan-stitch around center star. Make long stitches from center of star, following seam lines to sides. Sew button to center.

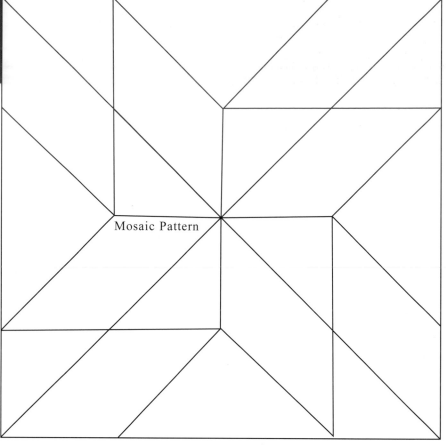

Mosaic Pattern

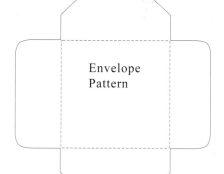

Envelope Pattern

Step 3

Adhere handmade paper piece to large sheet of heavy-weight card stock. Cut piece to fit card design. Enlarge and copy, then cut Envelope Pattern from heavy card stock. Center and adhere handmade paper with block to envelope. Using a stylus, score folds.

Step 4

Sew buttons on the front of envelope to secure closed.

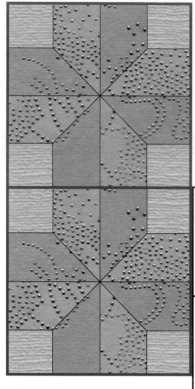

Victory Journal

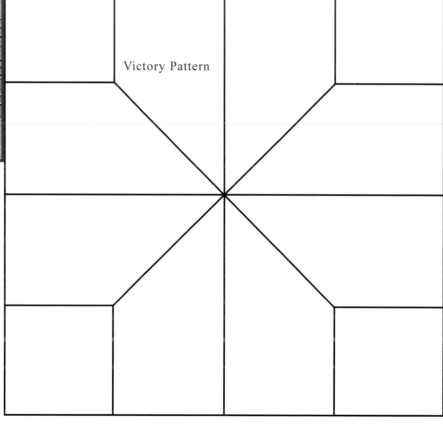

Victory Pattern

Step 1

Enlarge and copy Victory Pattern onto desired papers. Cut out and assemble pieces.

Step 2

Refer to Embroidery Stitches on pages 12–13. Herringbone-stitch over seam lines of quilt block. To prevent multistranded thread from unraveling when sewing, thread needle by passing a loop through needle eye and then passing needle tip through loop. Pull tight to form knot at needle eye.

Step 3

Adhere block to paper-covered journal.

Pocket
Scrapbook Page

			Twelve Square Pattern

Step 1

Enlarge and copy Twelve Square Pattern onto desired papers. Cut out and assemble pieces.

Step 2

Refer to Embroidery Stitches on pages 12–13. Feather-stitch over all connecting lines in block.

Step 3

Cut square ½" larger than block from background paper. Fold margin to the back and adhere. Blanket-stitch bottom and sides to scrapbook-sized piece of card stock. Whipstitch along top edge of block.

Step 4

Permit quilting friends to each sign a section. Store photographs of the group's activities in the pocket.

Hayes Corner Keepsake Box

Step 1

Enlarge and copy Hayes Corner Pattern onto desired papers. Cut out and assemble pieces.

Step 2

Cut one sheer fabric square slightly larger than square formed by two triangles. Place fabric on paper block. Using embroidery thread and sewing machine, straight-stitch ¼" seam around three sides of fabric. While still in machine, insert found objects under fabric. Continue sewing last side of fabric to secure found objects inside. Use a variety of other machine stitches to enhance seam lines in block.

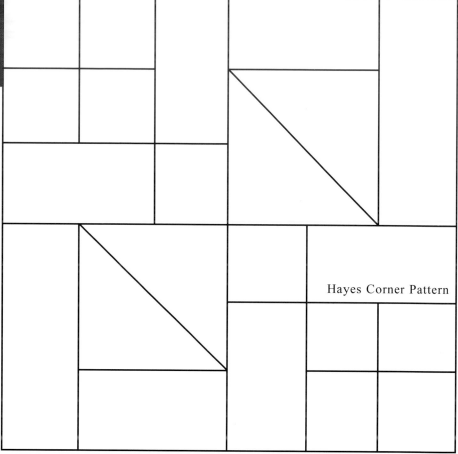

Hayes Corner Pattern

Step 3

Cut square ¾" larger than block from background paper. Stitch block to square.

Step 4

Mount block to box lid by piercing holes through block and lid. Using running stitch and double strands of same thread used on machine, hand-stitch around block. Secure knots on back with glue.

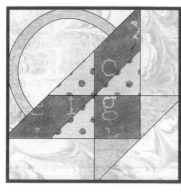

Basket Art

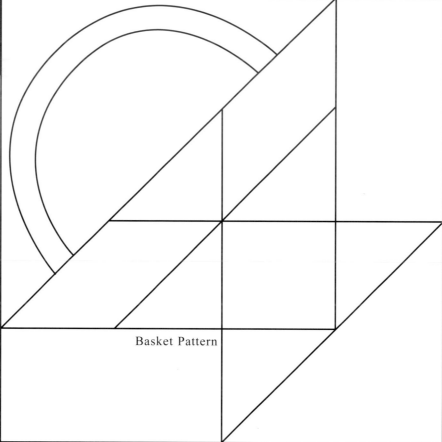

Basket Pattern

Step 1

Enlarge and copy Basket Pattern onto desired papers. Cut out and assemble pieces.

Step 2

Lay buttons, beads, ribbon, and crocheted flowers on quilt square to design the look you desire. Using beading needle, stitch on items one at a time. Secure items with seed beads if necessary.

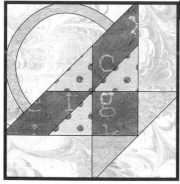

Step 3

Refer to Embroidery Stitches on pages 12–13. Using a chenille needle and silk ribbon, make several Japanese ribbon stitches to form leaves. Using three strands of floss, stitch a row of French knots in one of the bottom triangles. Using ribbon, come up from back on either side of diamond in body of basket. Tie into bow. Trim off excess ribbon.

Step 4

Wrap ribbon around basket handle. Make four straight stitches to resemble basket weave in the other bottom triangle. Adhere block to large sheet of wrapping paper with spray adhesive. Secure block to foam-core board and cut board to fit frame.

Duckling Envelope

Duckling Pattern

Step 1

Enlarge and copy Duckling Pattern onto desired papers. Cut out and assemble pieces.

Step 2

Refer to Embroidery Stitches on pages 12–13. Stitch long wheatear stitches around large inside triangles. When long slanted stitches are completed, finish the wheatear with yarn.

Step 3

Adhere block to natural handmade paper with spray adhesive. Using paintbrush and water, wet paper enough to easily tear for an uneven edge.

Step 4

Adhere block to heavy handmade paper folio.

Tips for Stitching on Paper:

Be aware that stitching on paper will dull the needle much quicker than will fabric.

Practice on a test sheet before stitching on a project.

Experiment with different types of threads.

Use a medium- to heavy-weight paper for best results. If using a thin paper, mount to another paper before stitching.

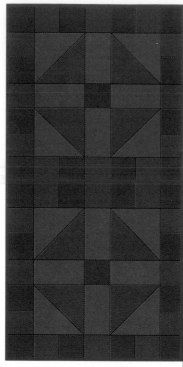

Lincoln's Platform

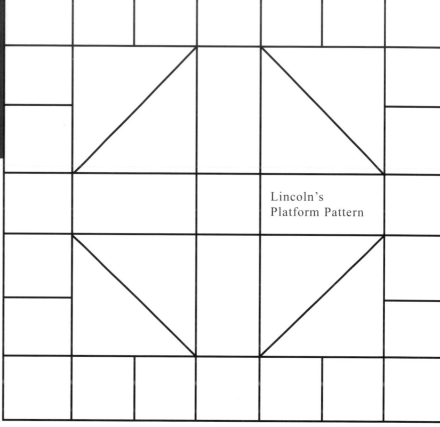

Lincoln's
Platform Pattern

Step 1

Enlarge and copy Lincoln's
Platform Pattern onto desired
papers. Cut out and assemble
all pieces.

Step 2

Cut card from card stock ½"
larger on three sides than the
block.

Step 3

Refer to Embroidery Stitches on pages 12–13. Using
Danish flower thread and chenille needle, stitch an
Algerian eye in center and corner squares. Stitch half-
lattice along outer edges and center vertical lines.
Stitch open fishbone along center horizontal lines.

Whirling Fish

Whirling
Fish
Pattern

Step 1

Enlarge and copy Whirling Fish Pattern onto desired papers. Cut out and assemble pieces.

Step 2

Refer to Embroidery Stitches on pages 12–13. Using metallic filament thread, sew zigzag chain around star. After stitching is completed, cut background from wrapping paper ¾" larger than block.

Step 3

Using beading needle and black beading thread, attach a copper disk and a bead to center of star. Knot to secure.

Step 4

Adhere block to wrapping paper with spray adhesive. Adhere block to card stock.

Sharon Glanville

Sharon traditionally creates designs with pen and ink, then brings them to life using a variety of color mediums. Her artistic pursuits have included photography, acrylic and watercolor painting, sketching whimsical characters as shown at left, and especially doodling for hours.

Through her varied experiences, and her unique illustrative process, she keeps her approach fresh by continuing to experiment with various mediums.

Sharon has always loved the glorious colors, interesting patterns, and endless beauty in the quilts her sister creates. By combining her love of quilting and her artistic illustrating abilities, she has created her own unique paper-quilting style.

110

Just as with traditional quilting, Sharon has found the fusion of patterns, colors, and textures with paper can be produced either by hand or with a sewing machine. Both methods provide an opportunity to bring to life her designs as well as traditional block patterns.

Sharon is often inspired by wandering through a fabric store and taking in the wide array of colors and patterns. She feels that possibilities are limited only by one's imagination.

She creates her designs in black ink then colors them with watercolors or permanent markers. A variety of smooth and textured papers are selected to add interest and depth. Even old greeting cards are beautiful when quilted together with twine, ribbon, or thread.

"Like all art forms, let your imagination be your guide. One of my favorite ways to embellish paper quilting is to use different textured, heavy pulp papers that can be cut and colored."

Sharon's Instructions

Sharon uses basic supplies for paper quilting and sewing that are commonly found around her home.

Suggested Supplies:

Black permanent ink pen, .18
Bristol 100 lb. paper (smooth surface)
Buttons, assorted
Craft glue
Decorative embellishments
Embroidery flosses, assorted
Eraser
Heavy pulp paper
Masking tape
Needles, assorted
Pencil
Permanent design markers
Ruler
Scissors
Sewing machine
Threads, assorted

Needle Types:

Sharps are strong, fine needles with round eyes, used for hand-sewing.

Embroidery or crewel needles—common sizes are from 1 to 10.

Darning needles—keep an assortment of sizes from 14 to 18.

Chenille needles—common sizes are from 18 to 24.

Needles & Threads

Sharon prefers a combination of machine and embroidery needles. When hand-stitching, she first pierces holes in the paper with a sewing machine needle. These needles are usually large, quite sharp, and have a top that can be easily held while piercing the holes for sewing. She follows up with an embroidery needle when quilting the design.

She prefers to use embroidery thread when quilting. There are numerous colors to choose from and, though the thread is thin, it is still quite strong.

Background Materials

Use your imagination when selecting materials. Consider items such as:

Card stock
Construction paper
Fabric
Handmade paper
Heavy pulp paper
Scrapbook paper
Wrapping paper

Tips from Designer:

Stay organized, so when a project idea hits or you have a few spare minutes to work, you will already have the necessary supplies at hand and your time will be better spent.

Keep adhesives and threads compatible with the papers to be used. A thin paper will be destroyed by a heavy-duty glue, just as a heavy paper will not be easy to work with if using a thin silk-like thread.

Sharon's Construction

Sharon brings her love of painting and drawing into her quilt designs. By designing and painting the papers to be quilted, Sharon finds the exact paper color and the compatible look she wants.

Step 1

Using a pencil and high-quality bristol paper, graph out a 6" square such as the Square Grid Diagram at right. Lightly mark inside of square in 1" sections. A ruler is a must for evenly aligning the design.

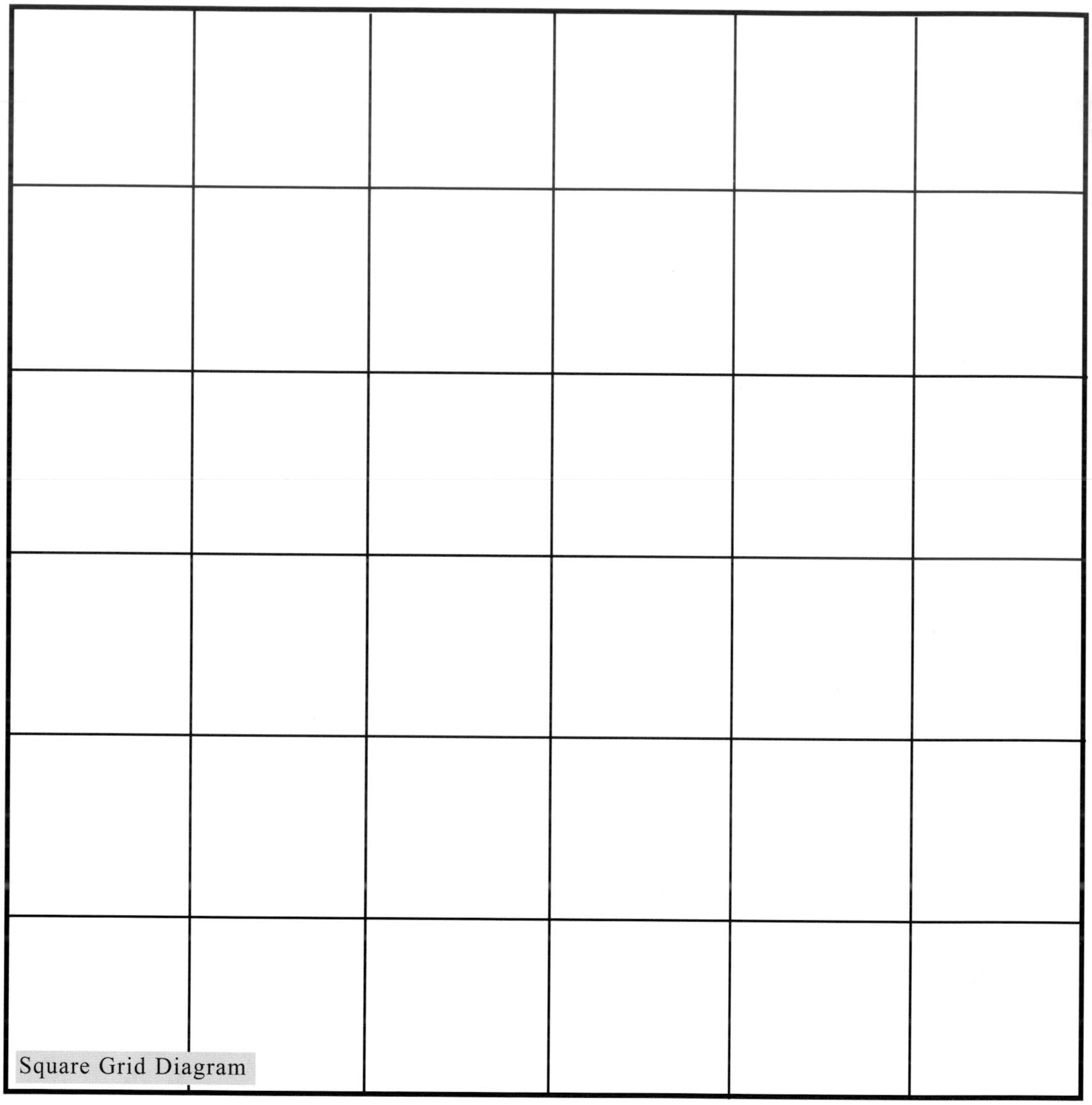

Square Grid Diagram

Triangle
Box
Pattern

3

Step 2

Enlarge and copy pattern, such as Triangle Box Pattern above, to fit a 6" block.

Step 3

Design each block with a variety of patterns. Using ink pen, go over design.

Step 4

Using watercolors or permanent markers, color in desired patterns.

Step 6

Add buttons or other decorative embellishments and use a variety of threads and twine to create texture and interest.

Step 5

Refer to Embroidery Stitches on pages 12–13. Use sewing machine or hand-stitch desired patterns onto blocks.

Step 7

Secure thread ends to avoid fraying. Note: The best method is to pull the final thread through the back, as you do traditionally, then secure with a piece of masking tape. The back of the block may look a bit messy with this method, but the end result has proved better than others I have tried.

House Block

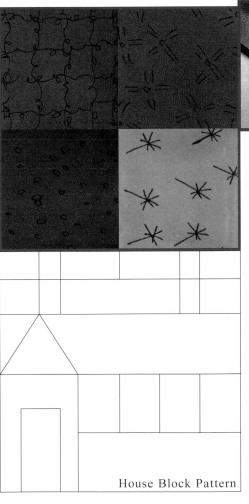

House Block Pattern

Step 1

Enlarge and copy House Block Pattern onto heavy pulp paper.
Design and color varied patterns in each quilt block.

Step 2

Refer to Embroidery Stitches on pages 12–13. Using a running
stitch and embroidery floss, stitch around outline of house and
around complete block. Sew on wooden buttons.

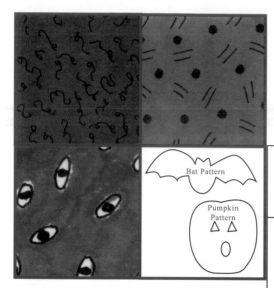

Halloween Block

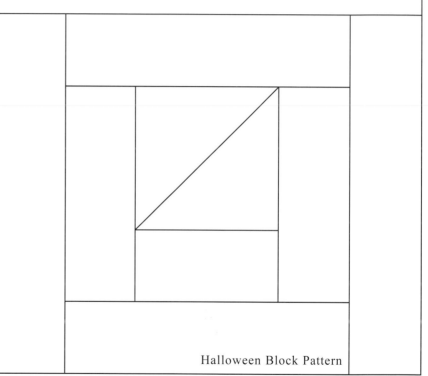

Halloween Block Pattern

Step 1

Enlarge and copy Halloween Block Pattern onto heavy pulp paper. Design and color varied patterns in each quilt block.

Step 2

Using sewing machine, sew small zigzag stitch inside the drawn seam lines. Sew perimeter with blanket stitch. To finish, run stitch off paper at end and secure with a hand-tied knot.

Step 3

Using Bat Pattern above, cut out bat from heavy pulp paper. Using Pumpkin Pattern above, cut out pumpkin from orange felt. Color with markers. Hand-tack bat and pumpkin onto block with small straight stitches.

Brooke

Don't forget
Halloween Party, October 31, 7 pm
RSVP

itch or a bad witch?

Earl

Finish Costume
Deliver Treat Bags
Homemade Root Beer Recipe

Star Block

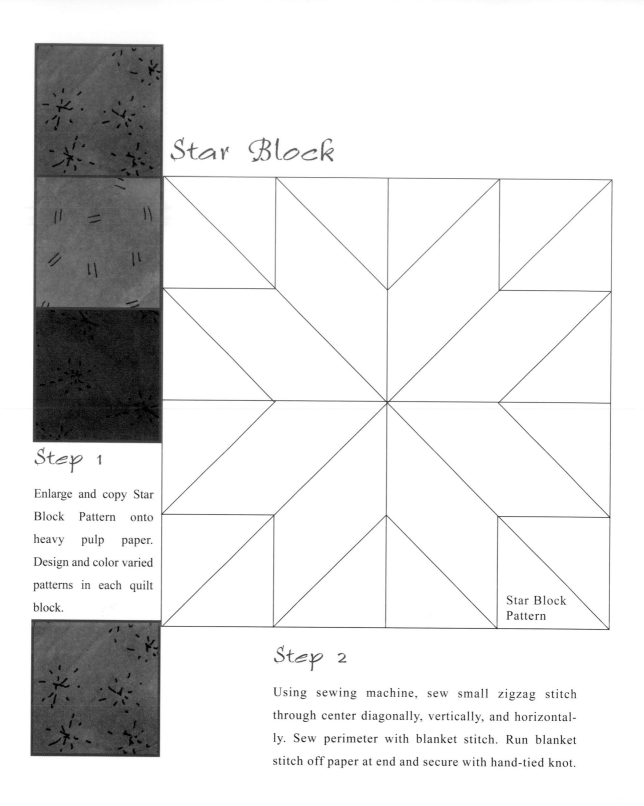

Star Block
Pattern

Step 1

Enlarge and copy Star Block Pattern onto heavy pulp paper. Design and color varied patterns in each quilt block.

Step 2

Using sewing machine, sew small zigzag stitch through center diagonally, vertically, and horizontally. Sew perimeter with blanket stitch. Run blanket stitch off paper at end and secure with hand-tied knot.

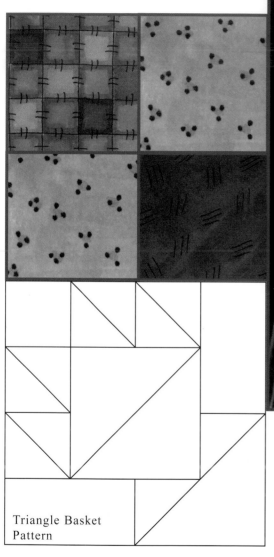

Triangle Basket
Pattern

Triangle Basket

Step 1

Enlarge and copy Triangle Basket Pattern onto heavy pulp paper. Design and color varied patterns in each quilt block.

Step 2

Secure embellishments with straight stitches at each corner.

Box Star

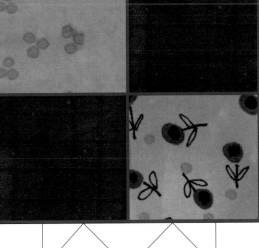

Box Star
Pattern

Step 1

Enlarge and copy Box Star Pattern onto heavy pulp paper.
Design and color varied patterns in each quilt block.

Step 2

Stitch through paper to secure metal star in center with knot.

Tree House

Tree House Pattern

Step 1

Enlarge and copy Tree House Pattern onto heavy pulp paper. Design and color varied patterns in each quilt block.

Step 2

Refer to Embroidery Stitches on pages 12–13. Using sewing machine, sew small zigzag stitch on inside seams. Hand-stitch perimeter with running stitch.

Step 3

Hand-stitch door with small straight stitches. Attach star in center with single straight stitch through center.

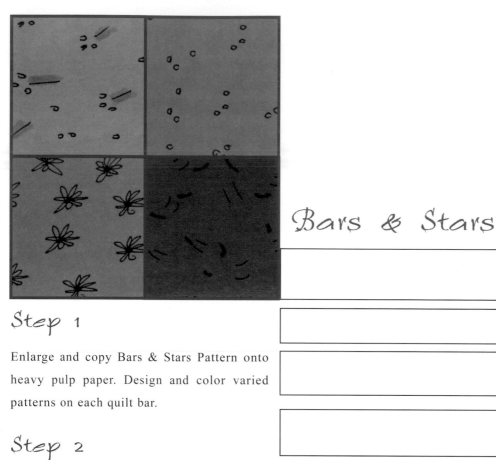

Bars & Stars

Bars & Stars Pattern

Step 1

Enlarge and copy Bars & Stars Pattern onto heavy pulp paper. Design and color varied patterns on each quilt bar.

Step 2

Using sewing machine, sew a decorative stitch on inside seams to secure bars.

Step 3

Using markers, color wooden cutouts. Lace twine through cutouts and tie with bow. Secure a mat around piece with masking tape.

Index

Conversion Chart

inches	mm	cm
1/8	3	0.3
1/4	6	0.6
3/8	13	1.3
1/2	16	1.6
5/8	19	1.9
3/4	22	2.2
7/8	25	2.5
1	32	3.2
1 1/4	38	3.8
1 1/2	44	4.4
2	51	5.1
2 1/2	64	6.4
3	76	7.6
3 1/2	89	8.9
4	102	10.2
4 1/2	114	11.4
5	127	12.7
6	152	15.2
7	178	17.8
8	203	20.3